16TH Nov. 1992.

To Ian

With Much Love on this special
Birthday.

From Ian & Esther.

RACING AND THE IRISH

Kooyonga (Warren O'Connor), trained near Ashbourne, County Meath, by Michael Kauntze, wins her third Group One race, the Coral-Eclipse Stakes at Sandown Park in July 1992

RACING AND THE IRISH

Sean Magee

Stanley Paul

LONDON

Stanley Paul & Co. Ltd

An imprint of Random House (UK) Ltd

20 Vauxhall Bridge Road, London SW1V 2SA

Random House Australia (Pty) Ltd
20 Alfred Street, Milsons Point, Sydney 2061

Random House New Zealand Limited
13 Poland Road, Glenfield, Auckland

Random House South Africa (Pty) Ltd
PO Box 337, Bergvlei 2012, South Africa

First published 1992

Set in 11/14 Garamond Light by
SX Composing Ltd, Rayleigh, Essex
Printed and bound in Great Britain by
Butler & Tanner, Frome and London

A catalogue record for this book is available from
the British Library

ISBN 0 09 174937 9

Photographic acknowledgements

The author and publishers would like to thank the following photographers and agencies for allowing them to use
their copyright photographs: Gerry Cranham pp. 9, 38, 47,
70-1, 74, 87, 95, 97, 103 (top), 109 (both), 114, 117, 129
(both), 133, 137, 138, 148; Caroline Norris pp. 22, 103 (bottom), 113, 130, 142, 156, 161; The Hulton Picture Company
pp. 46, 55, 58, 85, 90, 126, 127; George Selwyn frontispiece,
pp. 62, 67, 93, 159; Sport & General Press Agency pp. 79, 81,
82, 106; *The Observer* pp. 27, 34, 44; Mary Evans Picture
Library p.11; Illustrated London News Picture Library p.60;
Associated Press p.76; Press Association p.124; Pat Maxwell
p.145; Paul Ross p.165; Bernard Parkin p.152.

CONTENTS

PREFACE

THE STORY IS told of how a driver travelling through the Midwest of the USA stops in a remote town and enquires at the local store whether they could sell him a garlic. 'No,' apologises the proprietor, then calls after his departing customer – 'but I know what you mean.'

An element of 'No – but I know what you mean' dogs an author trying to pin down the nature of the special Irish affinity with horse racing. Everyone knows it exists, but few care to be specific about its social and cultural roots. The Irish have made an impact on world horse racing quite disproportionate to the size of their country. That is indisputable, and since analysis is much less fun than celebration – and 'a celebration' is what the publisher asked for – the simple aim of this book is to celebrate the achievements of the Irish in racing over the last half century.

But we must not get carried away by visions of Ireland as a paradise of rolling green pastures being quietly grazed by the cream of the world's Thoroughbreds, racecourses swarming with rubicund priests and pubs full of endearing old characters babbling about Arkle or Vincent O'Brien. In reality, the notion that the Irish are bound together by an obsessive love of racing is as bogus as that of their country as an idyll for motorists.

A volume of this size can do little more than scratch the surface of a large and fascinating topic. I can only hope to have the opportunity to dig deeper in the future.

Roddy Bloomfield of Stanley Paul Ltd commissioned this book under the reasonable assumption that anyone called Sean Magee must be an Irishman. When I confessed that, although of Irish extraction and named after the great jump jockey whose exploits sadly fall just outside the period of this book, I was born in England, he took this intelligence with singular good grace. To his colleague Dominique Shead, thanks for her supreme efficiency and assistance. Thanks also to Louise Speller and Lauren Clark, for making Stanley Paul a pleasure to work with.

For various kindnesses, I owe an especially affectionate debt to Lady Thomson – widow of Tom Dreaper – and to her husband Sir John Thomson. Information and help has been gratefully received from Richard Beadle, Ray Goddard, Chris Jones, Phillip Jones, Sir Rupert Mackeson, Richard Onslow, John Tyrrel, and Cheltenham racecourse. Gillian Bromley has yet again proved a tireless ally in the preparation of the text. The words to 'Arkle' by Dominic Behan are reproduced by kind permission of Coda Music Ltd.

By far the most enjoyable part of writing this book has been the visits to Ireland, where so many people have provided information or insights. I am particularly grateful to Dr and Mrs Vincent O'Brien for their hospitality and their comments on drafts of the text; likewise to Bob Lanigan at the Coolmore Stud; to Michael Osborne at the Kildangan Stud; to John Clarke at the Irish National Stud; to Michael and Eva Kauntze for hospitality and a personal introduction to my beloved Kooyonga; to Jim Dreaper; to Valerie Dreaper; to Finbarr Slattery; to Paddy and Maureen Mullins; to Arthur Moore; to Matt Mitchell at Irish Thoroughbred Marketing; to Richard Henry; to Valentine Lamb; to Caroline Norris; to Joe Collins; to Tony Sweeney; and especially to Raymond and Sheila Smith, for hospitality and all manner of other assistance.

I was reading the proofs of the chapter about Arkle when word came that Pat Taaffe had died. A few weeks earlier I had spent a memorable afternoon with this most kindly of jockeys at his home at Alasty, talking over the deeds of Arkle and so many other great horses he had ridden. It was a privilege to have met him.

Gail Sinclair's main claim to a close connection with the Turf is that some decades ago the youthful Jim Dreaper was the first boy ever to kiss her. I am greatly in her debt for this information, and for providing me with an Irish base at the Old Street Wine Bar in Malahide, of which she is the fearsome *propriétaire* and from which was launched much research for the last chapter of this book. I am especially grateful to Annie McNamara, Gordon Henderson and Alan and Cathy Griffin for their unselfish and unstinting efforts when tutoring me in the crack, and to Margaret Maher for that, for hospitality and for teaching me the words of 'The Mountains of Mourne'.

S.M.

BOOKS
I have benefited from the work of many other writers, including Irish Horse-racing *by John Welcome,* Horses, Lords and Racing Men *by Fergus A. D'Arcy,* The Horse in Ireland *by Brian Smith,* Between the Flags *by S. J. Watson,* The Irish Derby *by Guy St John Williams and Francis P. M. Hyland, and* Horse Racing, *edited by Finbarr Slattery – as well as books by Raymond Smith on Vincent O'Brien, Ivor Herbert on Vincent O'Brien, on Arkle and on other great chasers, Bryony Fuller on Tom Dreaper and Jonathan Powell on Monksfield.* The World of the Irish Horse *by Grania Willis was published too late for me to be able to steal its best stories, but is strongly recommended for those who wish to read more about the horse in Ireland.*

CHAPTER ONE

'A Sweet and Plentiful Grass'

Ireland and the Racehorse

Some three centuries before Nijinsky became the only Irish-trained horse to win the Triple Crown, a diplomat in the service of Charles II was deputed to examine ways in which the economy of Ireland could be improved. In *An Essay upon the Advancement of Trade in Ireland*, addressed to the Lord Lieutenant and published in 1673, Sir William Temple made much of the notion that one activity upon which the Irish should concentrate was the breeding of high-quality horses:

Horses in Ireland are a drug [no longer in demand], but might be improved to a commodity, not only of greater use at home, but also fit for exportation into other countries. The soil is of a sweet and plentiful grass, which will raise a large breed; and the hills, especially near the sea-coasts, are hard and rough and so fit to give them shape and breath and sound feet.

Sir William went further. To provide a testing ground for the new improved breed of Irish horse which would emerge from a more discriminating approach to breeding than had been the case hitherto, race meetings should be held in certain places for one week every year, with the king ('Old Rowley' himself, Charles II, but for

whom we would not have the Nell Gwyn Stakes) donating plates, one of £30, another of £20, 'for horses proved to be Irish-bred'. The racing-mad Charles II – the only reigning English monarch to have ridden a winner – was understandably sympathetic to such a scheme, giving 100 guineas as a prize for a King's Plate.

At the time this tentative move in the direction of organised horse racing in Ireland was made, forms of racing had already been taking place in the country for centuries.

The beginnings of the Irish identity with the horse are impossible to pin down accurately. Folk tales from the earliest period of Celtic civilisation tell how horses transported people across the water to the Otherworld, the life after death, and the horse regularly appears in ancient Irish lore. Racing horses is as old as the nation, and certainly took place between the ancient kings and tribal chiefs. But the first stirrings of horse races set up as public entertainment are to be found at the *aonach* – the fair, or, in one derivation, the 'contention of horses'. One such fair was held at 'The Curragh of the Liffey' – the Gaelic word *currech* denoting a place where horse races were run. A huge plain just outside Newbridge in County Kildare, as a training centre and racecourse The Curragh was to become the Irish equivalent of Newmarket.

This communal assembly was often located on the burial ground – reinforcing the idea of the horse bringing man to the Otherworld – and was an opportunity for a variety of activities, sporting, social, legal and commercial. The *aonach* was a public festival of renewal, and if the racing of horses was an integral part of it, that was not merely for entertainment. For part of the renewal process was the affirmation of your king's ability to ward off enemies, and he strove to exhibit his supremacy by possessing the winning horse. Brian Smith, in his book *The Horse in Ireland*, links ancient and modern when writing of the king at the races: 'Perhaps his subjects saw in the victory of a champion – like the crowds that gather at Cheltenham racecourse to cheer on an Arkle against a Mill House – their own triumph.' Perhaps, too, there was a more down-to-earth reason for jubilation, for the possession of the best horses could have a very direct bearing on the outcome of inter-tribal clashes.

The most significant of the early breeds of Irish horse was the 'hobby', a small but very tough and durable type which had originally been imported to Ireland from Spain. By the sixteenth century, the hobby was the fastest horse in the British Isles, and many crossed the Irish Sea to race in England, their domination waning only when the importation of Arab stallions at the end of the seventeenth century triggered the evolution of the Thoroughbred we know today.

The suggestions which Temple had proffered for the control of Irish racing had little immediate effect, and horse races at The Curragh continued to be held as a fairly haphazard adjunct to the fair. The Revolution in 1688 affected hopes of bringing rapid order to racing and breeding, but the sport revived early in the eighteenth century. In 1731 the *Dublin Intelligencer* reported:

Horse racing is become a great diversion in the country. The Commons of Ardmagh were threatened to be taken up for some public use, but the people of the town contrived to apply them to a greater advantage by making a horse-course round about them ... The company that

AT GALWAY RACES

There where the course is,
Delight makes all of one mind,
The riders upon the galloping horses,
The crowd that closes in behind:
We, too, had good attendance once,
Hearers and hearteners of the work;
Aye, horsemen for companions,
Before the merchant and the clerk
Breathed on the world with timid breath.
Sing on: somewhere at some new moon,
We'll learn that sleeping is not death,
Hearing the whole earth change its tune,
Its flesh being wild, and it again
Crying aloud as the racecourse is,
And we find hearteners among men
That ride upon horses.

W. B. YEATS

Nineteenth-century leppers

*comes to these races help to keep up the people's spirits by con-
suming their liquors – the chief manufacture of the place. The
Collector of Excise affirms that His Majesty's duty is visibly increased thereby.*

It was in the mid-eighteenth century that Ireland made a singular
contribution to the history of horse racing. Match races between
two horses and riders had been common for centuries, but a particularly Irish version was the 'pounding match', especially beloved
of the gentry in Clare, Roscommon and Galway. Lots would be
drawn to decide the leader, who would ride and jump his horse
across as difficult a stretch of country as he could hazard, and his
opponent had to follow, with victory going to the rider who first
'pounded' his opponent to a standstill. As a variation on such a
pounding match, in 1752 Mr Edmund Blake and Mr O'Callaghan
rode a match race over a line of country agreed in advance – from
Buttevant Church in County Cork to the spire of St Leger Church,
four and a half miles away.

Thus was born a new code of horse racing – steeplechasing: 'A
sort of racing', in the words of one English visitor, 'for which the
Paddies are particularly famous, in which, unless the rider has

pluck and his prad goodness, they cannot expect to get well home.'

The Jockey Club in England was founded around 1750, and it is usually assumed that its first Irish member, Thomas Conolly, called upon his knowledge and experience of that revered Newmarket institution in helping to set up the Irish equivalent, the Turf Club. Yet there is evidence that the idea was in fact transplanted to England from Ireland, where a version of the Jockey Club was in existence in the late 1740s. The first volume of the *Irish Racing Calendar* recorded results from 1790, but the Turf Club certainly existed at least six years earlier than that.

In 1807 the *Irish Racing Calendar* used the word 'steeplechase' to describe a match over six miles, and the cross-country code grew rapidly in popularity during the early years of the nineteenth century. Chasing was a hazardous business. In a race at Lismore the winner fell four times, the third horse home six times: 'In all twelve falls, but nobody killed.' And in a foretaste of those 'novelty bets' of recent years on which horses would get round in the Grand National – 'Betting: evens at starting there would be six falls.' John Welcome has noted how another English visitor described steeplechasing: 'This system of horsemanship, dangerous in the extreme, has become the favourite amusement of the young fox-hunters of the day,' and another writer in 1809 admired the Irish horses as 'the highest and the steadiest leapers in the world'.

In 1817 the Stewards of the Turf Club instituted a race at The Curragh which they hoped would match the prestige of the Derby at Epsom – first run in 1780 – but the O'Darby Stakes had to be abandoned, due to lack of support from owners and lack of interest from the public, after just eight runnings.

The visit of George IV to The Curragh on 31 August 1821 gave a significant boost to the status of the Turf Club and of racing in Ireland. It also suggested an unfortunate alternative meaning to the *currech* as a place of running, for the day before the proposed royal visit the king had a severe attack of diarrhoea. This was a pivotal moment in Irish racing history, and it is worth quoting in full the details supplied to the diarist Thomas Creevey by the Countess of Glengall:

On Wednesday last His Majesty was expected at The Curragh, but he gave a grand dinner the day before to the Knights and Todies of St Patrick, at which he showed evident signs of uneasiness in his Royal stomacher, and was thereby obligated to send an excuse early in the morning to his expectant worshippers, who were mounted cap-a-pied (with his Grace of Leinster at their tail) for the purpose of escorting the track of his royal wheels. Add to this, that the whole of the inhabitants of the South of Ireland from Bantry Bay, Cork and Cahir and the intermediate cities had assembled pêle-mêle on The Curragh to get a glimpse of the idol, where there was neither house nor tree to afford them shelter. The common labouring people had set off like mad beggars ... leaving their harvest (crying out to be cut) to the mercy of the wind and rain.

But lo! the wherry-go-nimbles, which had so unreasonably attacked the Royal stomach (for even kings are subject to these unkingly complaints), gave his Majesty full employment at the Phoenix Park, and the Duke of Leinster arrived at The Curragh with this direful intelligence.

Lord Portarlington and the other stewards, twelve in number, were assembled to receive this second St Patrick. They had spent near £5,000 in erecting a glass house and providing a suitable banquet for the Royal party. When, therefore, they were informed of the complaint which detained their promised guest, their grief was audible, but they were in some measure comforted by the assurance that if the castor oil (so liberally administered) was true to its office, he would come on Friday, the day but one after.

One of the Stewards stood forth with great solemnity in the august assembly of Managers and said, 'Gentlemen, I fear one thing has been omitted, which it appears may be an essential necessary; I mean a watercloset, and I humbly propose that artists may be forthwith summoned from Dublin to erect one before his arrival.' ... His Grace of Leinster volunteered to ride himself to town, twenty-three Irish miles, to bring down Mr Simmons, the Bramah of Dublin. His Grace's offer was thankfully accepted, and he rode off ventre à terre, and returned accompanied by the said artist ... Mr Simmons only asked instructions as to the dimensions and size which the Stewards wished to have for the seat and its appurtenances. Lord Mayo rose and observed that 'He conceived the usual dimensions would suffice as his Majesty, though corpulent, was finely tuned.' The Earl of Meath, who had the day before received the Blue Ribbon at his Majesty's hands, said 'That though his limbs were small, the contours of his person were round, and that he proposed that Mr Massey Dawson, the Member for Clonmel, should be measured as a certain criterion to go by.' Mr Massey Dawson declared his willingness to contribute by any means in his power. In twenty-four hours the machine &c. &c. were on the road to The Curragh, and a few hours more saw it placed in its niche. But lo! when the pump was tried a trifling oversight was discovered – no water was forthcoming except only that which poured from the heavens. . . .

The debate had just arrived at this stage when distant shouts were heard, and the Stewards flew to receive the Royal sufferer. A tall friend of ours preceded him upstairs, and the doctor, following close in his rear, took an opportunity of assuring the Stewards that nothing but his anxious wish to wait upon them could have induced his Majesty to journey so far under existing circumstances.

All the ceremonies of the reception being gone through, the horses started, but before they could arrive at the winning post his Majesty was obliged to bolt. His Grace of Leinster was called for, as he had undertaken to do the honours of the new erection – exeunt the Duke walking first with a white wand, then the King, and immediately behind the doctor. 'How fortunate' was immediately echoed round the room, nay round the course itself, and thanks were immediately voted to the Lord of Portarlington . . .

Temporarily, at any rate, delivered from the wherry-go-nimbles, the king returned to the sport, and before the end of the afternoon presented the Royal Whip, with a solid gold handle, to be run for annually: 'And as I wish to encourage the breed of strong horses in this country, you will take care to make the weights very heavy and that no horse younger than four years shall be permitted to run for it.' The Royal Whip is still run today, in modified form, though the pong from George IV's retiring house has long since wafted into the sweet air of Kildare.

In the wake of the royal visit, racing in Ireland prospered, though the process inevitably went into reverse after the Great Hunger of the 1840s and the mass emigration which followed the famine. But in the middle of the century the sport was given a real fillip by two exceptional horses: Birdcatcher and Harkaway.

Birdcatcher put up one of the great performances of Irish racing in the nineteenth century in the Peel Challenge Cup over a mile and three quarters at The Curragh in 1836. Taking the lead from the start, he was never headed and won by a distance described as 'over five hundred yards'. But his jockey was unable to pull him up once the winning post had been passed, and Birdcatcher bolted as far as the cavalry barracks at Newbridge, two miles away. As a stallion Birdcatcher did much to promote Irish bloodstock: he was the sire of the 1852 Derby winner Daniel O'Rourke and the grand-sire of Stockwell, one of the most important stallions of the nineteenth century.

The other great Irish racehorse of the time, Harkaway, was one of the few top-class horses to have been bred in Ulster. He won seventeen races in Ireland and eight in England, including the Goodwood Cup in 1838 and 1839, and beat Birdcatcher in the Northumberland Handicap at The Curragh in 1837.

The exploits of Harkaway as a racehorse in England and sub-sequently of Birdcatcher as a sire were spreading the word about the quality of Irish horses, and their growing reputation was to be boosted further by the great steeplechasing innovation of the mid-century: the Grand National. The precursor to the National proper was first run at Maghull, near Liverpool, in 1837, and the following year went to Sir William, owned, trained and ridden by an Irish-man in Allen McDonough. The first Irish winner of a Grand National at Aintree was Mathew in 1847, followed by Abd-El-Kader in 1850 and 1851. In 1850 the first three were all Irish bred, owned, trained and ridden.

Before these triumphs, however, and soon after the National had been established at Aintree, the Irish played their part in the chris-tening of two of the course's most famous fences. Tom Ferguson, owner of Harkaway, was riding in the 1839 event alongside one Captain Becher on Conrad when they came to the brook second time round. Just what happened is not known, but Ferguson carried on and Becher landed in the water, where his sodden pro-

An Irish Callcard for use in public telephone boxes. You can see why some Irish punters think their domestic racing is not as straight as it might be: number 3 is being scrubbed along towards the finish, while number 20, scarcely out of a back canter, is not being ridden to obtain the best possible placing . . .

nouncement 'It's damn cold stuff without brandy in it!' presaged the sponsorship of the great race by Martell. The other famous brook fence on the Grand National course, Valentine's, takes its name from the Irish-trained horse who put in a renowned cork-screw jump at that fence on his way to running third in 1840. So by mid century the Irish horse had clearly made a substantial impression on chasing in England, and the influence was spreading farther afield: St Leger, second to Mathew in the 1847 National, went on to become the first Irish horse to win the Grand Steeplechase de Paris.

The Irish Derby was first run in 1866, over an extended one and three quarter miles. Six years later the distance was reduced to twelve furlongs to match the Derby at Epsom, though it was not until the huge injection of prize money from the Irish Sweeps in 1962 that the race started to achieve the international status it enjoys today.

But the influence of Ireland on Flat racing overseas was steadily increasing in the latter half of the nineteenth century, a process stimulated by three more famous Irish-bred horses. Barcaldine was unbeaten in Ireland and won several big races in England, notably the Northumberland Plate carrying 9st 10lb, and Bendigo won the first ever running of the Eclipse Stakes in 1886, as well as the Jubilee Handicap, the Lincoln Handicap, the Hardwicke Stakes and the Champion Stakes – the last of these, in 1887, just two days after running second in the Cesarewitch under 9st 7lb. Gallinule won almost £2,000 as a two-year-old in 1886 but could not be kept sound enough to win again. However, he proved outstanding at stud, heading the list of winning stallions in England in 1904 and 1907. Among his offspring was Pretty Polly, winner of nineteen of her twenty-one races (including three Classics) and possibly the greatest racemare of all time, who was bred by Major Eustace Loder at his Eyrefield Stud, not far from The Curragh.

The year 1888 saw the inaugural meeting at Leopardstown, Ireland's first enclosed course and a landmark in the process of the modernisation of Irish racing. Leopardstown was modelled on Sandown Park, which had become the first English 'park' course when it opened its gates in 1875 and enjoyed great success since: as on the opening day at Sandown, a huge crowd turned up at Foxrock in suburban Dublin for the first Leopardstown meeting to discover that the course was scarcely prepared for such an invasion, and in the resulting chaos a wholesale riot was only narrowly averted. The course at Phoenix Park, modelled on London's Hurst Park, was opened in 1902 (and closed in October 1990).

Irish horses took ten of the eleven Grand Nationals between 1889 and 1899 (including the two won by Manifesto); curiously, the only non-Irish winner during that period was an English-bred named Father O'Flynn. Round the turn of the century the importance of the Irish in English Flat racing continued to grow, and with the great Galtee More we see that influence spreading further afield. Bred in County Limerick by John Gubbins, Galtee More was put into training with Sam Darling at Beckhampton and won three important races as a two-year-old, then at three in 1897 won the Two Thousand Guineas with ease, the Derby at 4-1 on, the Prince of Wales's Stakes at Ascot, the Sandringham Cup at Sandown, the St Leger (10-1 on) and the Sandown Park Foal Stakes. Galtee More was thus the first Irish-bred horse to win the Triple Crown, and John Gubbins the first Irishman to be leading owner in Britain. Gubbins sold the horse to the government of Russia, and from there Galtee More moved to Germany: in both countries he sired top racehorses. Galtee More's half brother Ard Patrick, also owned and bred by John Gubbins and trained by Sam Darling, won the Derby in 1902 and beat Sceptre in the famous 1903 Eclipse Stakes.

In 1907 the Derby was won for the first time by an Irish-trained horse – Orby, owned by 'Boss' Croker and trained at his Glencairn Stud in Ireland by Colonel Frederick MacCabe. The entry on Croker in the *Biographical Encyclopaedia of British Flat Racing* (by Roger Mortimer, Richard Onslow and Peter Willett) is worth quoting:

Mr Richard ('Boss') Croker was born in Ireland and emigrated to America as a child. Tough, ruthless, self-opinionated and entirely devoid of moral scruples, he was cut out for success in American politics and in fact made a fortune for himself as the powerful and totally corrupt 'Boss of Tammany Hall'. When at last things got a trifle too warm for him in America, he transferred himself and his money to England, eventually settling in Ireland with a Cherokee second wife 50 years his junior. Taking to the Turf, he found his theory that American horses were of necessity faster than English ones extremely expensive...

After Orby had won the Derby, Croker sent a case of champagne to the Stewards of the Turf Club. If they suspected an ulterior motive they had reason: Croker then offered to endow the Irish Derby with enough money to make it as valuable as the Epsom race – on condition that he be elected a member of the Club. The gesture fell flat: the champagne bubbles had not befuddled the Stewards' brains sufficiently for the offer to merit serious consideration.

But in the lower reaches of society there was much rejoicing that an Irish-trained horse had finally won the major English Classic, and an old lady was moved to exclaim to trainer Frederick MacCabe: 'Thank God and you, sir, we have lived to see a Catholic horse win the Derby!'

Orby went on to become the first horse to complete the double of the Derby and Irish Derby.

One Irish-bred horse who left a lasting mark on the English racing scene just before the First World War was The Tetrarch, 'The Spotted Wonder' who is often held to be the fastest horse ever seen. He was bred at the Straffan Stud, County Kildare, and returned to stud in Ireland after a meteoric racing career in England, where he ran only as a two-year-old in 1913 and was unbeaten in seven races, including the Coventry Stakes at Royal Ascot and the Champagne Stakes at Doncaster. The Tetrarch stood as a stallion at Mount Juliet, County Kilkenny, at the stud which belonged to his owner Major Dermot McCalmont, but the horse's distinct lack of interest in sex made him a less influential stallion than he might have been. None the less he was champion sire in 1919 and got three St Leger winners as well as the brilliantly fast Tetratema and Mumtaz Mahal.

The Tetrarch in his old age at the Ballylinch Stud, Mount Juliet, shortly before his death in 1935 at twenty-four. In his final years part of his daily routine was to be ridden to the local post office with the letters

Racing continued throughout the war and insurrection, though often on a reduced scale, and the political upheaval of the struggle for independence inevitably had an impact on the sport. In 1917 police and nationalists clashed at Listowel following the annual races there, and the effects of the railway strike and coal shortages caused meetings to be abandoned. In July 1920 Frank Brooke, the Turf Club's Senior Steward, was assassinated in the offices of the Dublin and South Eastern Railway, of which he was chairman – possibly on account of his having been a Privy Counsellor and adviser to Lord French.

Between the wars Flat racing in Ireland went through a dismal patch, but Irish-breds continued to dominate jumping – notably Easter Hero, winner of the Cheltenham Gold Cup in 1929 and 1930, and Golden Miller, five times winner of the Gold Cup (1932-6) and still the only horse ever to win the Gold Cup and the Grand National in the same year (1934). Golden Miller was born on a farm near the village of Drumree, in County Meath, where Laurence Geraghty kept cattle and one or two hunter broodmares and boarded 'the Miller's' dam, Miller's Pride. Golden Miller's sire Goldcourt had never run, and was standing at a fee of five guineas when his most famous son was conceived. After the Miller became famous, the fee went up to eight guineas. Then there was the dual

Grand National winner Reynoldstown and the 1937 National hero Royal Mail, and plenty more. Indeed, sixteen of the twenty-two Grand Nationals run between 1919 and 1940 were won by Irish-bred horses.

As we will see when considering the career of Prince Regent, racing in neutral Ireland stuttered on during the Second World War, despite occasional hiccoughs, and jumping in particular prospered – though petrol shortages had an effect on the mobility of horses, and overseas challenges were out of the question.

In 1945 came a crucial moment in the history of racing in Ireland with the creation of the Racing Board, the brainchild of Joe McGrath, one of the most influential figures in the history of Irish racing: an early leader of the IRA and later a government minister, he was a leading owner and breeder (winning the 1951 Derby at Epsom with Arctic Prince) and founder of the Irish Hospitals Sweepstakes. The aim of the Board was to improve racing and breeding by operating the on-course Tote and by extracting a levy from on-course bookmakers, and to complement the legislative powers of the Turf Club – with whom the Board, once up and running, was able to maintain a mutually beneficial working relationship.

The other big date in the post-war history of racing in Ireland is 1962, when, again through the vision of Joe McGrath, the prize money for the Irish Derby was massively boosted through £30,000 from McGrath's Hospitals Trust. The first Irish Sweeps Derby was worth £50,027 to the winner, as opposed to the £34,786 which Vincent O'Brien's Larkspur had netted when winning that year at Epsom. Larkspur was in the field at The Curragh but could finish only fourth behind the French colt Tambourine II, who beat Arctic Storm by a short head in front of a crowd of over 40,000. Irish racing had truly joined the international set, and since that 1962 running ten winners of the Derby at Epsom have gone on to land the big prize at The Curragh: Santa Claus (1964), Nijinsky (1970), Grundy (1975), The Minstrel (1977), Shirley Heights (1978), Troy (1979), Shergar (1981), Shahrastani (1986), Kahyasi (1988) and Generous (1991).

Since the end of the war the racing world has seen a succession of great horses sent out from Ireland by great trainers and ridden by great jockeys. Arkle, Ballymoss and Nijinsky, Dreaper, O'Brien and Prendergast, Molony and Taaffe have all left an indelible Irish impression on the sport. Irish trainers have pushed back the frontiers in the top American races. And, most promising for the future prosperity of the racing and breeding industries in the country, many of the world's top stallions now stand in Ireland, picking at the sweet and plentiful grass.

The luscious grass is only one of the elements which make Ireland such an outstandingly good country in which to be a horse. The fabled closeness of the Irish to the horse, and the consequent importance of the Irish contribution to horse racing, results from a combination of factors. These may be broadly divided into the physical and the social.

Top of the list of the physical benefits which Ireland bestows is limestone. Much of the country is rich in this rock, which sits under a good depth of clay, especially the areas around Counties Tipperary, Meath and Kildare where so many of the top studs are to be found. Limestone and trace minerals build good bone in horses, and with the moist climate ensuring lush pasture and weather which rarely turns very cold, Ireland is the ideal place to rear youngstock. Horses take in minerals through grazing and through their intake of water, which like the grass is rich in limestone and calcium. Thus it is that the typical Irish horse has particularly fine bone, and as a consequence is likely to be tough and sound.

The landscape itself plays a part as well, for the particular ability of Irish-bred horses to jump well owes much to the ditches and banks which characterise the country's terrain, and to which many future steeplechasers are introduced in the hunting field.

The social bond between the Irish and racing is less straightforward. It is claimed that there are more horses per head of population in Ireland than in any other country in the world. Certainly it is the case that a greater proportion of the population than in more industrialised countries grows up close to the land, and therefore close to farm animals. Most farmers keep a mare or two and engage in the cycle of breeding and foaling, and thus the rudiments of horsemanship, as well as an ease and confidence in the presence of horses, are widely bred into Irish children. Cattle and horses form an important part of a farming livelihood, and from the cradle up the talk is of horses. Hunting, too, is a major form of rural recreation, which in its turn fosters good horsemanship.

But times are changing. Urban development is on the increase, the small family farm is under continuing pressure, and the notion that all the Irish are horse-mad is wide of the mark. For the majority of the population, horse racing is a matter of complete indifference. Yet evidence of the traditional closeness with the horse is still around. A horse is to be found on the obverse side of a twenty-pence piece. (When the old half-crown coin bore a similar equine portrait, some canny operators started selling them during the convalescence of Arkle after his Kempton Park injury at ten shillings a time – four times face value – as 'Medals of Arkle'.) A Callcard for use on public telephones advertises Irish horse racing: this is part of the culture, it is saying, part of the attraction of the country. There are stories of horses being reared in lofty flats in tower blocks and being brought down in the lift to exercise – or are they apocryphal tales, urban legends reflecting the town-dwelling Irishman's urge to hold on to his rural roots?

The delights of Killarney

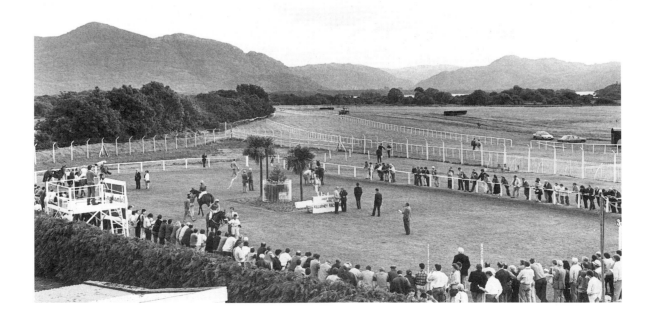

Those rural roots are strong, and the influence of the Irish horse has been felt throughout history – and not just in racing. In Buttevant, immortalised as the starting point of the first steeple-chase, 600 horses were once sold at the annual Cahirmee Fair who would perform the Charge of the Light Brigade. Before that, a horse sold at the Fair became Napoleon's famous charger Marengo.

Ireland's greatest artists have paid homage to the importance of the horse and racing in the nation's life. James Joyce's *Ulysses*, no less, takes place on an important race day – Ascot Gold Cup day, 1904:

He told them of the race. The flag fell and, huuh, off, scamper, the mare ran out freshly with O. Madden up. She was leading the field: all hearts were beating. Even Phyllis could not contain herself. She waved her scarf and cried: Huzzah! Sceptre wins! But in the straight on the run home when all were in close order the dark horse Throwaway drew level, reached, outstripped her. All was lost now. Phyllis was silent: her eyes were sad anenomes. Juno, she cried, I am undone.

'At Galway Races', one of W. B. Yeats's finest short poems, sings the praises of racing and racing people. And the painting 'Before the Start', a brooding depiction of Galway races in 1915 by the poet's brother Jack B. Yeats, hangs in Dublin's National Gallery.

The Galway track which inspired the Yeatses is one of twenty-seven racecourses in Ireland, including two north of the border: as far as racing is concerned the division between Eire and Northern Ireland does not exist. Ireland has one racecourse per (roughly) 185,000 population, compared with Great Britain's one per 920,000. Of those twenty-seven, only The Curragh and Laytown – where racing takes place one day a year on the sands – confine themselves to Flat only, and Kilbeggan now stages only National Hunt. The rest are for both codes, though jumping is much more popular with racegoers.

And British racing is much more popular with punters in the betting shops than the home product: not much more than a tenth of the money bet off-course is placed on Irish races. There is a perception, right or wrong, that the overseas sport is more competitive – perhaps more 'straight' – than racing in Ireland, and thus a more reliable betting medium.

Irish racing has its problems. Although courses such as The Curragh, Leopardstown and Fairyhouse have fine modern facilities, some of the smaller country courses are in varying degrees of dilapidation and in sore need of an injection of cash. Irish racing receives no direct cut from off-course betting: only on-course bets generate the levy for the sport, though the government does provide an annual grant for the racing and breeding industries. At the lower end of the prize-money scale Ireland is a better proposition for owners than Britain, but the country stages few races of top international importance. Irish trainers find it increasingly difficult to buy the best horses in the sales rings in the face of stiff competition from their English and French counterparts for Flat horses, and from English trainers for the best jumping prospects. Several Irish yards have horses for the Maktoum brothers, for instance, but the best of these tend to be sent to their English or French trainers. Of the nineteen Irish Classics run between the 1989 Two Thousand Guineas and the 1992 Oaks, only three went to Irish-trained horses: Petite Ile (John Oxx) in the 1989 St Leger, Kooyonga (Michael Kauntze) in the 1991 One Thousand, and St Jovite (Jim Bolger) in the 1992 Derby. The home team simply does not have enough ammunition to withstand the challengers regularly. Yet on some foreign fronts Ireland is doing conspicuously well: Kooyonga and St Jovite lit up Sandown Park and Ascot in July 1992, while three of the first four Italian Classics that year fell to Irish-trained horses – Treasure Hope (Jim Bolger) in the Italian equivalent of the One Thousand Guineas, Ivyanna (Jim Bolger again) in the Oaks d'Italia and In A Tiff (Dermot Weld) in the Derby Italiano. *Bravissimo!*

But the purpose of this book is not to analyse the current racing scene in Ireland, rather to chronicle some of the remarkable achievements of the country's horses and horsemen. And the only rightful place to start is with Himself.

CHAPTER TWO

ARKLE ARKLE ARKLE ARKLE ARKLE

AT THE HEIGHT of the Swinging Sixties the columnist Angus McGill offered readers of the London *Evening Standard* his 'box of pin-ups', in response to a book recently published by the photographer David Bailey. McGill's list was:

MARIA CALLAS   ARKLE   CHARLES WILSON
PICASSO   THE QUEEN   *(of Great Train*
MARGOT FONTEYN   VIVIEN LEIGH   *Robbery infame)*
NUBAR GULBENKIAN   A BEATLE   EL CORDOBES
YURI GAGARIN   *(John Lennon was*
JACKIE KENNEDY   *the one photographed)*

The description of Arkle read: 'The world's greatest steeplechaser, magnificent, unbeatable, one of the great aristocrats of our time. Anyone misguided enough to complain that horses aren't people is not a true-born Englishman.'

Nor, more to the point, a true-born Irishman. For no horse was ever identified more closely with his homeland than Arkle. Bred by a small-time breeder in County Dublin and bought by the County Cork-born widow of an English aristocrat, trained by the greatest of Irish jumping trainers, ridden to all his big victories by a famous Irish jockey and idolised by the Irish racing public, the horse epitomised Irishness in racing and has remained a potent symbol of the quality of the Irish influence on the sport.

Arkle was, and is, a true national hero. Guinness was an essential part of his diet. His skeleton is the prize exhibit at the Irish Horse Museum at the National Stud in Tully, County Kildare. His image adorns playing cards, a chewing-gum card, a tea-towel in 'Pure Irish Linen', the eighteen-pence Irish stamp issued in 1981. The bar named in his honour is the traditional meeting place for the Irish at Cheltenham; on the same course, Doris Lindner's superb statue of him looks out, ears pricked, over the paddock. And more than two decades since his death, Irish racing fans need little prompting to talk over his exploits and live again the glory days of the Sixties, when according to a ruddy-faced fellow interviewed by a plummy-voiced reporter for BBC television, talk in every pub in Ireland was 'ArkleArkleArkleArkleArkle – that's all – it's Arkle the whole way.'

So much has been written about this peerless horse that an apology for reciting again his extraordinary achievements and extolling his qualities might be considered appropriate. But none is needed here, for Arkle's life and career represent the quintessence of Irishness in racing. At the height of his fame fan letters addressed to 'Arkle, Ireland' unerringly found their way to him. The envelope of one such letter from Belfast was decorated with the plea:

Postie, postie, don't go slow
Go like ARKLE – go man go

And as successive generations of racehorses provide performances to be matched against his in some eternal form-book, so his record has been strengthened by the test of time.

Reduced to its simplest terms, that record was that Arkle ran in twenty-six steeplechases and won twenty-two of them, including the Cheltenham Gold Cup three times, the Leopardstown Chase three times, the Hennessy Gold Cup twice, the King George VI Chase, the Irish Grand National and the Whitbread Gold Cup. In all he won twenty-seven of his thirty-five races. He never fell in a race. Only six horses ever beat him over fences, and his superiority over his contemporaries was so great that the rules of handicapping in Ireland had to be changed to accommodate his pre-eminence: the 'A' handicap set the weights to be carried if Arkle ran, the 'B' handicap ranked all the other entries in the race without regard to Arkle, thus preserving the desired differences between the runners should Arkle not take part.

It takes an exceptional athlete to bring about a change in the rules of his sport. Arkle was truly a horse apart.

★ ★ ★

Born at the Ballymacoll Stud, County Meath, at 3.30 a.m. on 19 April 1957, Arkle was bred by Mrs Mary Baker, a widow who kept three or four mares on her farm at Malahow House in the north of County Dublin. This is an area rich in breeding associations: Easter Hero, Golden Miller and Reynoldstown were all bred nearby.

Arkle's sire Archive had failed to win a race but boasted a superb pedigree, being by Nearco out of Book Law, who had won the St Leger in 1927 after finishing second in the One Thousand Guineas and Oaks. Archive was standing at a fee of just 48 guineas when visited by Arkle's dam, Bright Cherry. Trained by Tom Dreaper and regularly ridden by Pat Taaffe, Bright Cherry had

Himself

been a good chaser in her racing days, and there was a further Dreaper connection with Arkle's maternal granddam Greenogue Princess, whom Tom had trained and had ridden in point-to-points, winning one (he reported of that race that 'I had a fellow standing by the second last fence to catch her when she fell and put me up again' – though she did not fall). These links with Arkle's forebears were to stand Dreaper in good stead within a few years of the horse's birth.

Arkle was reared at Malahow, where as a yearling he disgraced himself. Jumping a fence in pursuit of two fillies, he tore his fore-leg on a strand of barbed wire and sustained a wound which required forty stitches and the scar of which he bore for the rest of his life. Later that year he was gelded, then in August 1960 was sent as a three-year-old to Goffs sales at Ballsbridge, where he was sold for 1,150 guineas to Anne, Duchess of Westminster, the former Miss Nancy Sullivan of County Cork. The Duchess took her new acquisition and her other purchase from that sale, a handsome three-year-old by Flamenco, across to her estate in Cheshire where they were broken in and given time to thrive and mature before being put into training.

The Archive gelding was named Arkle after a mountain on the Duchess's Sutherland estates in Scotland, and after a year in Cheshire it was time for life to get serious. Tom Dreaper came across to choose which of the Duchess's two four-year-olds would go into training with him at Greenogue, and it was now that his ties with the Arkle family played their part. Although the other horse, named Brae Flame, was much the more imposing of the pair, Dreaper decided that blood was thicker than water and opted for Arkle. Brae Flame went to the Duchess's other Irish trainer, Willie O'Grady, and ran just once before leg problems brought about a premature retirement.

Pat Taaffe has memorably recorded his impression of Arkle upon the horse's arrival at Greenogue: 'He was a great gaunt thing. You could have driven a wheelbarrow through his hind legs.' And Arkle probably wouldn't have objected had you tried to do so, as already he was displaying that kindness of temperament which would become such a prominent aspect of his personality. On a more down-to-earth level, for head lad Paddy Murray, Arkle was

ARKLE

It happened in the springtime of the year of sixty-
four
When Englishmen were making pounds and fivers by
the score.
He beat them on the hollows, he beat them on the
jumps
A pair of fancy fetlocks, well he showed them all the
bumps.

He's English, he's English, English as you've seen
A little bit of Arab stock and more from Stephen's
Green
Take a look at Mill House, throw out your chest
with pride
He's the greatest steeplechaser on the English
countryside

Then a quiet man called Dreaper living in the
Emerald Isle
Said, 'That horse of yours called Mill House surely
shows a bit of style.
But I've a little fella, and Arkle is his name.
Put your money where you put your mouth and
then we'll play the game.'

Well the racing English gentlemen laughed till fit to
burst,
'You tried before, Tom Dreaper, and then you came
off worst.
If you think your horse can beat us, you're running
short on brains.
It's Mill House that you're talking of and not those
beastly Danes.'

Arkle now is five to two, Mill House is money on,
They're off! and dare believe I do, the champion has
it won.
There are other horses in the race to test the great
chap's might,
But dearie me! it's plain to see the rest are out of
sight.

There are three more fences now to go, he leads by
twenty lengths.
Brave Arkle's putting in a show – poor chap, he's all
but spent!
Mill House sweeps on majestically, great glory in
each stride,
He's the greatest horse undoubtedly within the whole
world wide.

Two to go, still he comes, cutting down the lead,
He's beaten bar the shouting, he hasn't got the speed.
They're on the run-up to the last, 'My God! can he
hold out?
Look behind you, Willie Robinson, man what are
you about?'

They're at the last and over, Pat Taaffe has more in
hand.
He's passing England's Mill House, the finest in the
land.
'My God, he has us beaten, what can we English
say?
The ground was wrong, the distance long, too early
in the day.'

DOMINIC BEHAN

the worst looking of the 1961 intake of four-year-olds: 'He was un-
furnished. And he moved bad.'

The notion at Greenogue that Arkle was nothing out of the
ordinary was not dispelled by his first race. On 9 December 1961
he ran in the Lough Ennel Maiden Plate for amateur riders at Mullingar, over 2 miles 1 furlong 160 yards and worth £133 to the
winner. Ridden by Mark Hely-Hutchinson (who has the distinction
of being the only man to have ridden Arkle and not won on him),
the four-year-old gelding started at 5-1 and ran on through beaten
horses to finish a respectable, though hardly earth-shattering, third.
Less than three weeks later, on Boxing Day, he ran in his second

Arkle and Paddy Woods make their way from the Greenogue stables to the gallops

bumper, the two-mile Greystones Maiden Flat Race at Leopardstown. Again ridden by Mark Hely-Hutchinson and again starting at 5-1, he finished fourth. Ahead of him in third place was a grey mare making her debut – Flying Wild, of whom Arkle would be seeing more.

The Bective Novice Hurdle at Navan on 20 January 1962 represented a significant step up in distance for Arkle at three miles, and a noticeable step up in class. For among his twenty-six opponents was his stable companion Kerforo, winner of her previous three races, the choice of stable jockey Pat Taaffe and hot favourite at even money. Despite the favourable impression of his first two outings, Arkle, ridden by Liam McLoughlin, was completely unfancied at 20-1. This was Arkle's first race over obstacles and he was given plenty of time to see what he was doing, so it was no surprise to his connections to find him in the rear in the early stages. As the race reached its climax attention focused on Pat Taaffe and Kerforo as they fought a losing battle with Blunts Cross, and then, to the general amazement of Tom Dreaper and his wife Betty in the stand, the unconsidered form of Arkle came sweeping up the outside to win by one and a half lengths. As Tom Dreaper came down to greet his unexpected winner he turned to his wife and said: 'Do you know, I think we've got something there!' The most glorious list of wins in National Hunt history had begun.

Pat Taaffe took over the ride for Arkle's next race, a two-mile hurdle at Naas in March 1962, and duly won at 2-1 favourite. But Arkle's two subsequent outings in the 1961-2 season failed to maintain the improvement – unplaced and fourth under Liam McLoughlin in hurdles at Baldoyle and Fairyhouse.

The 1962-3 season which was to thrust Arkle to the verge of stardom began with victories in a hurdle at Dundalk and in the President's Hurdle at Gowran Park. Then it was time to move up to the steeplechasing for which all his previous racing had been a solid education.

Arkle's first chase came not in Ireland but in England, at the course with which his name will for ever be especially identified – Cheltenham. It was a bold move on Tom Dreaper's part to introduce his protégé to chasing on a course where the fences have always been stiff, but a calculated one: he knew that his young charge could be something special, so why not drop him in at the deep end?

A measure of reputation had preceded Arkle, as he started favourite at 11-8 (having touched even money), with the second favourite Jomsviking going off at 11-2. The confidence was not misplaced. Arkle took the lead three fences out and swiftly drew away to record a twenty-length victory over Billy Bumps. It was becoming clear that this horse could indeed be something out of the ordinary, and sights were set on a return trip to Cheltenham in March for the Broadway Chase (nowadays the Sun Alliance Chase), the top race of the season for staying novice chasers.

After a prep race over two miles at Leopardstown, which he won with ease, Arkle arrived at Cheltenham looking like an Irish banker for the first day of the big meeting. A famously fierce English winter having severely curtailed the preparation of the home team, it was expected that the Irish raiders would have the fitness edge, and Arkle was sent off the 9-4 on favourite for the Broadway Chase. At the third last he was vying for the lead with Brasher and Jomsviking, and then, in the graphic words of John Lawrence (now Lord Oaksey) in *Horse and Hound*, he 'simply shot from between the two English horses like a cherry stone from a schoolboy's fingers' and strode up the hill – in going officially described as 'v. soft' – to win by twenty lengths.

It was a brilliant performance, but understandable thoughts in the Dreaper camp of lifting the Gold Cup at the following year's meeting were tempered just two days later when Mill House hammered Fortria by twelve lengths to win the 1963 running.

Mill House was six, the same age as Arkle and of no less

promise. The Gold Cup was only his sixth chase, and he had won four. More to the point, at Cheltenham the mammoth stride and massive jumping which jockey Willie Robinson had conjured from Mill House's huge frame had demolished a field of much more experienced horses. Notions that Mill House was the best chaser since Golden Miller in the 1930s were by no means fanciful.

Thus was the stage set for the most exciting period of steeplechasing in living memory. Mill House and Arkle were both brilliant young horses. Both seemed invincible, and both attracted fervent partisan support. The manner in which the supporters of Mill House and of Arkle divided into separate camps, neither hearing of defeat, provided the true spice of the clashes between the two and a telling insight into how the racing public perceives the national identity of its heroes.

Arkle was the 'Irish' champion, no doubt about that: owner, trainer, jockey, breeding – all Irish. Mill House presented some ambiguity. Bred in Ireland (he had been broken and ridden to his first victory by none other than Pat Taaffe), his regular jockey was the Irishman Willie Robinson, but the decisive element was his trainer. Never mind Mill House's breeding or jockey – he was trained in Lambourn by the great Fulke Walwyn, and that made him the English champion.

Jockeys Taaffe and Robinson were close friends, which added another dimension to the rivalry. After Mill House had been sold to go to England, Taaffe, familiar as he was with the young giant, wrote to Willie Robinson: 'You'll be up on the best horse in Britain – quite possibly the world.' After winning at Cheltenham on Arkle's chasing debut he sent a correction – 'You are now up on the *second* best horse in the world.' The two jockeys agreed that whenever Arkle and Mill House met, the winning jockey would buy the loser a consolation prize.

The first meeting was to be the Hennessy Gold Cup on 30 November 1963, and the racing world bubbled with anticipation as the day came nearer.

Since their respective Cheltenham heroics that spring Mill House had had one race, winning the Mandarin Chase at Newbury in April, and Arkle four, winding up the 1963 spring campaign with victories in valuable chases at Fairyhouse (the Power Gold Cup) and Punchestown – thus recording seven wins from seven runs that season – and opening the next term by winning a Flat race at Navan and the Carey's Cottage Chase at Gowran Park.

For Mill House, who was conceding Arkle five pounds, the Hennessy was his seasonal debut, but none the less he went off the 15-8 favourite, with Arkle 5-2 and Duke Of York at 8-1 next best of the ten runners.

On a dismal and foggy afternoon, Mill House led early on and still had a convincing advantage over his rivals turning for home with four fences to jump. Peering into the gloom, spectators in the stands could scarcely see how Arkle was making significant progress at the fourth last, but the television cameras showed him creeping up on Mill House and going every bit as well. At the third last Pat Taaffe asked Arkle to start his challenge, but the cameras lingering on that fence – the final open ditch – missed the crucial moment of the race as the Irish horse, having jumped well, slipped on landing and passed the initiative back to the big horse.

Arkle could not recover, and Mill House powered over the last two and emerged from the fog to an ecstatic welcome from his supporters. Happy Spring moved up to take second place, and although Arkle rallied on the run-in he could do no better than third.

The champion Mill House had put the upstart Arkle firmly in his place, and, as far as the English were concerned, that was all there was to it. Mill House was confirmed as the best chaser since Golden Miller, and the protestations about Arkle's slip at the third last could be safely ignored as so much Irish babbling. Arkle fans could make as many excuses as they liked, but Mill House had been a convincing winner.

There were precious few neutral observers around that day, but all save the most blindly partisan Mill House supporters had to admit that the Hennessy had been less than fully conclusive, and the result served only to heighten anticipation of the real showdown in the Cheltenham Gold Cup four months later.

Mill House went on to win the King George VI Chase at Kempton Park on Boxing Day; over the water on the same afternoon Arkle won the Christmas Handicap Chase at Leopardstown. At the end of January, Arkle took the Thyestes Chase at Gowran Park, and completed his Gold Cup preparation by lifting the Leopardstown Chase in mid-February, four days before Mill House won the Gainsborough Chase at Sandown Park. The only horse to offer Arkle a serious challenge at Leopardstown was the grey mare Flying Wild, whom he had encountered in the second race of his life and who before the end of 1964 would have joined the select group of horses ever to have beaten him in a steeplechase.

So Mill House had two races between the Hennessy and Cheltenham, Arkle three, and neither tasted defeat. No chinks were appearing in either's armour, and as the day of the Gold Cup drew closer and the build-up grew more intense, the partisan fervour melted down to an atavistic English–Irish rivalry. There were just two other runners, Pas Seul, winner of the Gold Cup in 1960, and the good chaser King's Nephew completing the quartet. But they were never in more than a very minor supporting role, as was anticipated by the betting: 13-8 on Mill House, 7-4 Arkle, 20-1 King's Nephew, 50-1 Pas Seul.

On a typical cold March day at Cheltenham, bright sunshine alternating with flurries of snow, the race lived up to its billing.

Setting a powerful pace, Mill House led Arkle for the first circuit, and by the top of the hill on the second Pas Seul and King's Nephew had fallen away. But Arkle remained effortlessly in his rival's slipstream as they hammered downhill for the last time, and to delirious Irish fans in the stands it was only a matter of when

The moment of truth: Arkle and Pat Taaffe leave Mill House and Willie Robinson behind at the last in the 1964 Cheltenham Gold Cup

Taaffe would ask him to go on. Mill House still held a marginal advantage at the second last but it was clearly on sufferance, and on the turn into the straight Arkle swept into the lead, popped over the final fence two lengths to the good and scurried up the hill to win by five lengths.

Those few seconds in which Arkle passed Mill House at the climax of the 1964 Cheltenham Gold Cup and quickened away up to the winning post provided Ireland with its greatest single occasion in racing history. Here was a horse with Ireland stamped right through him putting to flight the aspirations of the English contender. A champion needs a challenger to test his mettle, and Arkle had put his challenger firmly in place. The old enemy had been comprehensively routed, and the rapture which rang out around Cheltenham that cold March afternoon was rooted in fierce national pride. Here was the Irish love of the horse made vocal in the presence of its greatest champion.

A drop of Guinness, courtesy of head lad Paddy Murray

Arkle returned to Ireland a national hero. On the day following the Gold Cup the road leading to Greenogue was clogged with the cars of worshippers come to pay homage. 'Nobody enjoyed it more than he did,' recalls Betty Dreaper: 'He adored it.' The newspapers sang his praises, and his demolition of Mill House was properly enshrined in Irish legend through the medium of song.

For a true emblem of what Arkle meant to the Irish, you need look no farther than the stirring ballad 'Arkle', composed and recorded by Dominic Behan. A gleeful lampoon of the confidence of the 'racing English gentlemen' who puff up Mill House and mock the aspirations of the Irish ('You tried before, Tom Dreaper, and then you came off worst'), Behan's song climaxes with the English panic when Mill House is challenged ('Look behind you, Willie Robinson, man what are you about?') and closes with a list of English excuses for the Big Horse's defeat. The core of the song is a celebration of putting one over on the English, of having the last laugh. If Gladiateur, the first French-bred winner of the Derby in 1865, was 'the Avenger of Waterloo', Arkle's victory in the 1964 Gold Cup likewise dealt an ancient enemy a wounding blow.

Old enmities die hard; so do old friendships, and Pat Taaffe kept his side of the bargain by purchasing the air tickets for Willie Robinson's honeymoon!

It was now that Arkle was paid the ultimate compliment that a sport can offer its participants – the rules being changed to accommodate one competitor's abnormal ability. It was not unheard of in the dim and distant past of steeplechasing for the conditions of a race to be framed specifically to exclude one horse: Lottery, winner of the Grand National in 1839, was barred from one event on account of his superiority, and in another his owner was expected to pay four times the entry fee levied on his rivals. But with Arkle the problem was a more general one. How could the weights allotted in a handicap have any meaning if one horse so comprehensively outstripped all the others in the race that his superiority, in terms of weight, spanned most or even all of the range of the handicap?

This was before the days of the 'long handicap', the current flexible system of amending the weights to be carried if the horses at the top of the handicap do not run. Before the alteration, Arkle's presence in a handicap effectively ruined it as such, for were he not to run, the rest would be huddled together at the foot of the weights and thus would have to run without the differentials which are the essence of handicapping.

Following the Gold Cup it was clear that Arkle was towards two stone superior to any of his contemporaries. As just one example of his pre-eminence, consider Flying Wild. In the Leopardstown Chase, she had carried 10st 2lb and received twenty-six pounds from Arkle, who beat her carrying 12st. In her previous race Flying Wild had carried 11st 9lb to victory in the valuable and very competitive Stone's Ginger Wine Chase at Sandown Park. Arkle was too good: and something had to be done.

The Stewards of the Irish National Hunt Steeplechase Committee came up with the solution that if the top weight in any handicap were weighted a stone or more higher than the second top weight, the handicapper was to frame a second set of weights, excluding the horse originally top-weighted. This method was first used for the 1964 Irish Grand National at Fairyhouse, Arkle's next race after that first Gold Cup, but the 'B' handicap was not on that occasion needed, as Arkle ran. He carried 12st. Next in the handicap was Flying Wild with 10st, but it was another tough Irish mare, Height O'Fashion (9st 12lb), who made Arkle work hard for victory by one and a quarter lengths.

Arkle spent the summer at the Duchess of Westminster's estate at Bryanstown, near Maynooth, then returned to training. By now he was a mature animal, and the ungainly youngster had developed into a superbly made horse. Much has been made of the depth of Arkle's ribcage (confirmed by his skeleton in the Irish Horse Museum), evidence of a massive heart and lungs, but the physical characteristics which linger in the memory of Arkle at his prime are his high, proud head carriage, and his extraordinary ears, which when pricked all but touched. And as the horse grew into his role of national hero, so the stories grew of what a true gentleman he was. As kind as could be at home, he was sublimely tolerant of visiting admirers being given a leg up for a few paces around the yard, and had a particular fondness for children. The story of how he retrieved for young Valerie Dreaper a ball which had found its way into his box during a game in the yard, and

Summertime, and the living is easy: Arkle on holiday with Anne, Duchess of Westminster at Bryanstown

Arkle before the 1964 Hennessy Gold Cup at Newbury

dropped it at her feet like a dog, is as much a part of the Arkle legend as many of his races.

Yet for all his sweet nature, Arkle was the supreme athlete, and after winning the Carey's Cottage Chase at Gowran Park in October 1964 he was faced with one of his stiffest tests in his next race against Mill House.

Although in numerical terms the 1964 Hennessy was the decider – the score going into the race being one apiece – most people knew that the Gold Cup had furnished conclusive proof of Arkle's superiority over his old rival. There had been possible excuses for Fulke Walwyn's charge (as Behan's song had satirically attested) but the feeling was growing that Arkle was not just something special – he was a freak.

The 1964 Hennessy Gold Cup was the last occasion on which Arkle started at odds against. Carrying 12st 7lb and giving Mill House three pounds, he went off the 5-4 favourite, with his main rival 13-8 and the Queen Mother's fine chaser The Rip at 8-1 the only other runner to start shorter than 20-1.

Mill House had not run previously that season, but his supporters' hopes were raised when Arkle, who had been expected to track his rival and then beat him for speed – as in the Gold Cup –

took on Mill House. What happened is crisply summarised in Pat Taaffe's autobiography:

On that day I rode Arkle the way I would ride no other horse. I let him dictate the tactics, absolutely confident that he would pick the right ones. So when he went to the front jumping alongside Mill House, I made no effort to check him. I am sure that he wanted to prove that he could outjump this king of jumpers and establish his own supremacy.

He began by matching Mill House jump for jump. If Mill House put in a big one, Arkle would put in an even bigger. It was heroic stuff and the crowd had eyes only for these two.

At the cross fence approaching the straight Arkle started to leave Mill House behind, and the Big Horse's spirit seemed to evaporate. Early in the straight he was struggling, and it was left to another Irish-trained horse, Ferry Boat, to try to get to Arkle – to no avail. At the second last Arkle clipped the top of the fence and screwed on landing, but the error scarcely disturbed his relentless gallop, and he came home by ten lengths from Ferry Boat, with The Rip running on to take third place and Mill House finishing desperately tired in fourth.

Arkle was now unarguably in a class of his own, and John Lawrence did not mince words the following week in *Horse and Hound*:

Since Messrs Blake and O'Callaghan set off to race from Buttevant Church to St Leger Steeple 212 years ago, thousands of men and women all over Great Britain and Ireland have worked and schemed and dreamed to produce the perfect 'chaser.

From time to time their dreams have been close to fulfilment. Perhaps, who knows, they were fulfilled. Cloister, Manifesto, Jerry M, Easter Hero, Golden Miller and Prince Regent – all these and other deathless names have kindled in men's hearts the self-same fire that burnt so bright at Newbury last Saturday afternoon.

Comparisons are pointless. All one can say without fear of contradiction is that no horse – certainly no seven-year-old – has ever looked more the complete, final, flawless answer than the Duchess of Westminster's Arkle.

By the end of the 1964-5 season the ghosts of the famous chasers listed by John Lawrence (all, be it noted without surprise, bred in Ireland) had to give best to Arkle – with the exception of Golden Miller, whose supporters maintained (and still maintain) a dogged defence of his superiority.

Seven days after the Hennessy win Arkle went to Cheltenham for the Massey-Ferguson Gold Cup over two miles five furlongs, a trip distinctly on the short side for him. He finished third carrying 12st 10lb, but his defeat by Flying Wild and Buona Notte, receiving thirty-two and twenty-six pounds respectively and beaten a short head and a length, was one of his most heroic performances. Having been headed just before the last fence, Arkle was catching the leading pair at the line, and Pat Taaffe believed that had he waited before going for home, he might just have caught Flying Wild up the hill. Never mind: it was still a magnificent effort.

Arkle resumed his winning ways the following February, with victory in the Leopardstown Chase the prologue to a second Gold Cup, in which he simply drew away from Mill House approaching the last fence – 'like a sports car ... as though he's just changed gear', as Peter O'Sullevan put it in his BBC commentary.

Next stop was the Whitbread Gold Cup at Sandown Park. Arkle carried 12st 7lb, conceding at least two and half stone to the best of his rivals. Brasher, who had won the Scottish National at Bogside two weeks earlier and was ridden by Jimmy FitzGerald, took Arkle on down the far side on the second circuit, but had no answer when Pat Taaffe pressed the accelerator going to the last fence. Arkle won by five lengths.

Arkle now belonged to all Ireland, and one of his summer duties was to appear at the Dublin Horse Show where, ridden round the ring by Pat Taaffe, he would graciously accept the obeisance of his fans. It was often said of Arkle that he loved playing up to the crowd – and said not only by sentiment-touched idolaters but by those closest to him in the yard and on the course.

His connections noticed that as a new season approached he would start to become fretful at home, so they adopted the ritual of boxing him up and taking him to a nearby racecourse – on a non-raceday – where he would be given an hour to remind himself of the track atmosphere, and perhaps be popped over a couple of fences. Which done, he would go home and resume his customary calm demeanour.

Arkle's first race of the 1965-6 season was, in terms of pure quality, possibly the greatest of the lot. In the Gallaher Gold Cup, a valuable sponsored handicap at Sandown Park in November 1965, Arkle faced six opponents – including Mill House. It was the fifth time the pair had met, and although the intense rivalry of two years previously had long been defused by Arkle's evident superiority, a weight difference of sixteen pounds seemed to offer Mill House a real chance.

But if any such impression was an illusion, Mill House at least played a leading role again in one of the greatest chases of the modern period. Having been applauded by the crowd out of the parade ring and on to the course, Arkle and Mill House roused the spectators to yet greater heights of ecstasy as between them they turned in an unprecedented display of jumping. Initially the running was made by Mill House, ridden for the first time by David Nicholson as Willie Robinson was injured, then Arkle took it up passing the stands at the end of the first circuit, then Mill House regained the lead along the back straight. The Big Horse kept up his gallop just like the champion he had been ('David was egging me on,' recalled Pat Taaffe), and starting the long run round towards the straight he lengthened his stride to go four lengths clear and present the distinct possibility that at last he would start to pay Arkle back for repeated humiliations.

But Arkle had other ideas. In the matter of five, maybe six strides he had engaged another gear and accelerated past his rival with such sublime ease that he went from being four lengths down to five lengths up in a few seconds and without any apparent pushing from his jockey. It would have been an almost incredible burst of speed from any horse in any race, but coming towards the end of a three-mile chase from a horse carrying 12st 7lb and conceding sixteen pounds to a Gold Cup winner, it beggared belief.

'I asked him to do more that day,' said Pat Taaffe – and having set Arkle alight he proceeded to pump him over the last three fences and up the hill to such effect that he broke the course record for the distance by no less than eleven seconds.

It was a staggering performance, as Quintin Gilbey in the *Sporting Chronicle* acknowledged: 'Races may come and go, but the Gallaher Gold Cup of 1965 will be talked about as long as the men and women of this country take pleasure from the spectacle of great horses battling it out over fences on a winter's day.'

Back in Ireland Arkle's status as folk hero was rock solid, as is testified by a newspaper article written by one Terry Wogan:

I often think that it's a great thing that we have racehorses in this country, otherwise we'd never win anything at all. I'll admit that we are glorious in defeat; why wouldn't we? We've had lots of practice. But Arkle actually wins, and wins, and wins. It's a pity we can't decorate him for all the money he brings into the country, as Queen Elizabeth did with the Beatles.

Arkle then won a second Hennessy, beating Freddie (to whom he conceded 2st 4lb) by fifteen lengths. Next came the King George VI Chase at Kempton (a race marred by the death of the great two-mile chaser Dunkirk), and the 1966 account was opened with a third Leopardstown Chase.

The 1966 Cheltenham Gold Cup was run on St Patrick's Day, in honour of which occasion a sprig of shamrock was lodged in Arkle's browband. If this was supposed to bestow some sort of saintly protection on the horse it certainly did its job, for at the fence in front of the stands on the first circuit Arkle made an almighty blunder, simply failing to rise at the obstacle and crashing through to draw horrified gasps from the spectators. It was the worst jumping error he ever made, but it delayed his triumphal progress not a jot – though Michael Scudamore on Dormant, more in hope than in expectation, called to Pat Taaffe: 'He'll fall yet!' Arkle jumped the next fence like a gazelle and proceeded to win by thirty lengths from Dormant at odds of 10-1 on, the shortest price he ever started and the shortest price ever returned in the Cheltenham Gold Cup.

By the middle of 1966, the world was at Arkle's feet. He was in his prime at only nine years old, had not been beaten for almost two years, and was clearly invincible in conditions races and effectively unbeatable in handicaps. What worlds were there left for him to conquer? Not the Grand National, for one. His owner had made it perfectly clear that the risks inherent in that race – especially loose horses – ruled out her ever being tempted to enter him. This introduced a trappy problem for those who insisted Arkle was undoubtedly a greater chaser than Golden Miller, for supporters of the Miller could claim that not only had their champion won the Gold Cup five times, he had won the National as well and was (in the mid 1960s) the only horse ever to have won both races. For their part, Arkle's fans could say that he was more superior to his contemporaries than Golden Miller had ever been, and more consistently brilliant. It wasn't *his* fault he'd never have the chance to win the National, and given time he would surely equal or even beat Golden Miller's Gold Cup haul.

Such comparisons were purely academic, but they passed the time until Arkle – now simply known to the Irish public as 'Himself' – should reappear on a racecourse.

When he did so, it was for his fourth consecutive Hennessy Gold Cup. He had not run since Cheltenham and had had a training setback through a small injury incurred when schooling over hurdles. Moreover, he was carrying 12st 7lb and as usual giving lumps of weight away to good horses – 2st to Freddie, 2st 5lb to What A Myth, 2st 7lb to Stalbridge Colonist. Victory was not a foregone conclusion, and he started an uneasy favourite at 6-4 on.

Arkle led up the straight but approaching the last fence Stan Mellor on Stalbridge Colonist was riding like a man possessed, driving the grey along in Pat Taaffe's wake. After the last fence Mellor thrust his mount into the lead, and taking advantage of his huge weight concession Stalbridge Colonist went a couple of lengths up, but then Arkle's indomitable courage asserted itself and – as in his last defeat in the Massey-Ferguson – he started to rally. At the line he was only half a length down.

Defeated but not diminished – that was the general verdict on Arkle's performance, an impression underlined when Stalbridge Colonist went on to narrow defeats in the Cheltenham Gold Cup in 1967 (second to Woodland Venture, beaten three quarters of a length) and 1968 (third to Fort Leney and The Laird, beaten a neck

Stan Mellor roars the grey Stalbridge Colonist past Arkle on the run-in of the 1966 Hennessy Gold Cup

and a length).

Arkle 'decisively readjusted his crown' (in the words of the *Sporting Life*) by carrying 12st 7lb to an easy victory in the the SGB Chase at Ascot (though Pat Taaffe had sensed that his action was inexplicably a little amiss in the race), then headed for Kempton Park for a second King George VI Chase.

With Tom Dreaper staying in Ireland, Pat Taaffe travelled to London with Betty Dreaper and her son Jim. Boxing Day itself, a Monday, produced frost and the Kempton card was postponed. Pat Taaffe and Jim Dreaper went off to Highbury to watch Arsenal play Southampton; Betty Dreaper went to the Festival Hall for a performance of the *Nutcracker Suite*. There was nothing to suggest that the King George – now to be run on the Tuesday, 27 December – would be anything other than one more exhibition round.

Arkle faced six opponents. He started at 9-2 on, with the useful young horse Woodland Venture next best at 6-1 and Dormant, who had beaten Mill House in the 1964 Whitbread when receiving three stone and had finished a distance behind Arkle when second in the 1965 King George, 10-1. (Among the other runners was a horse named Foinavon, who had previously been owned by the Duchess of Westminster and trained by Tom Dreaper, and whose date with the history books was only a few months away.)

The early stages of the race were uneventful. Arkle hit the guard rail on the take-off side of the fourteenth fence hard but sailed merrily on. Down the back straight on the second circuit Woodland Venture took on Arkle and was continuing to press him hard coming up the straight; then he fell at the second last, leaving Arkle set for a simple – if not particularly impressive – victory. But, oddly, Dormant, in receipt of twenty-one pounds from Arkle, was gradually closing. Arkle jumped the last clumsily and up the run-in was like a car rapidly running out of petrol. His action was going, and suddenly the unthinkable was about to happen.

It did. Dormant, driven along by Jeff King, caught him just before the line and won by a length.

Arkle was very lame when he came back, and practically crippled by the time he reached the unsaddling enclosure. Veterinary examination soon revealed that he had cracked the pedal bone in his off-fore hoof. It is not possible to know whether, as many thought, this happened at the second fence in the King George or at the last open ditch, or whether either mistake exacerbated an injury sustained in the SGB Chase. Whatever the cause, Arkle had broken a bone in his hoof, and might never run again.

He remained until the end of February in his box at Kempton Park, where he was bombarded with get-well cards, presents and visitors. The notion that Arkle was a gift from God was not dented by a letter to Betty Dreaper from the Cathedral Presbytery in Waterford:

Please permit me to join the many thousands who so sincerely sympathise with Mr Dreaper and yourself on the great tragedy that has befallen your great hero and ours. Excuse the word 'ours' but, as you know so well, in every corner of Ireland there are many who regard Arkle as their own in some way.

And a card received by the injured Arkle displayed the grace and courtesy of an old rival:

Get well soon

The convalescing Arkle and his companion Nellie lark around at Bryanstown

Dear Arkle

I was so sorry to hear about your recent injury at Kempton Park.

Ironically, I have only just recovered from a series of injuries, and I am only now back at my best. I was so looking forward to racing against you at Cheltenham and I think, with all due respect, I might have beaten you, as I am in tip-top condition now.

Wishing you a very speedy recovery, and looking forward to seeing you up and about and racing soon,

Yours faithfully,

Mill House

After continuing his convalescence on the Duchess's Irish estate, in a straw-padded barn and with a donkey for a companion, in October 1967 he returned to Greenogue. Hopes that he might run again rose and fell. Possible comeback races came and went, but he never gave the old feel to Pat Taaffe, who felt that he no longer really enjoyed jumping, and the decision formally to retire him became inevitable. On 9 October 1968 came the official announcement that Arkle would not race again.

He was gone but not forgotten, and appearances at the Horse of the Year Show in October 1969 (when the band played 'There'll Never Be Another You') raised the Wembley roof. But he was growing increasingly stiff, and when Pat Taaffe went to visit his old friend at Bryanstown in May 1970 Arkle was moving only with great difficulty. Taaffe alerted the Duchess, who flew from England to see her great horse one last time, and on 31 May 1970, at the age of thirteen, he was put down.

The skeleton of Arkle at the Irish Horse Museum, Tully, County Kildare

★ ★ ★

And that is the story of Arkle.

In telling it over and over since his racing career was brought to its untimely end, many have commented on the horse's great good fortune in his human associates. His owner appreciated that a steeplechaser needs time to develop and mature rather than be rushed into racing. His trainer embraced the same philosophy of patience and absolutely refused to wander from it, and – very much an element in the Arkle story – ran a stable peopled with the staff to carry through that philosophy. His jockey was a strong but sympathetic horseman who knew when to try to control Arkle's early headstrong impulses and when to let the horse have his way. His doting Irish public knew a great horse when they saw one.

These people all had their affinity with horses bred into them in Ireland, and the story of Arkle brings together all that makes the Irish relationship with the horse and with racing so remarkable.

His skeleton may adorn the Museum, but his memory lives on in Ireland wherever the talk is of racing.

ArkleArkleArkleArkleArkle – that's all – it's Arkle the whole way.

CHAPTER THREE

THE LEPPERS

ARKLE WAS NOT the first Tom Dreaper chaser to captivate the public. During the Second World War, with a severe petrol shortage curtailing transport, Dreaper had his horses walked to race meetings (or, for far-flung courses, the railway station), following behind in a pony and trap which contained the tack, feed and other necessaries for the day's racing. For Leopardstown meetings the horses would walk the seventeen miles or so from Kilsallaghan, north of Dublin, to the racecourse at the southern end of the city, through O'Connell Street. On one such occasion the string arrived at a busy crossroads and Dreaper asked a policeman to hold up the traffic for the horses to cross.

'Is Prince Regent there?', asked the policeman.

'He is.'

'Right. I'll stop the whole lot of traffic, both ways.'

And he did.

As with Arkle, the key factor dictating whether a horse is perceived by the racing public as being Irish is not so much its breeding as its trainer. Arkle and Prince Regent possessed that essential 'Irishness' through all their connections and associations. Dawn Run and Monksfield had it in a similar way, and it is much more likely to be found in National Hunt racing than on the Flat.

Jumping lies deeper in the Irish racing spirit than the Flat. Perhaps because of the closeness of much of the racing community to the hunting field, it is the jumpers – 'the leppers' – which raise the temperature, and which produce most of the best stories. It is no coincidence that of Irish racecourses, apart from the one day a year on the sands at Laytown, only The Curragh is exclusively for Flat racing. And jumping takes place round the year: the racegoers demand it.

Flat racing is too serious, goes the argument; for the best of the crack, bring on the leppers!

★   ★   ★

It was not until after Arkle had won his second Cheltenham Gold Cup that Tom Dreaper was prepared to concede that the Duchess of Westminster's great chaser was as good as an earlier inhabitant of Greenogue, the 1946 Gold Cup winner **Prince Regent**. Until then their trainer had judged Prince Regent just the better, but as Arkle's achievements piled up he would admit: 'Well, perhaps they *were* just about equal.'

Prince Regent was by one of the great Irish jumping sires, My Prince (also sire of Easter Hero and the Grand National winners Reynoldstown, Gregalach and Royal Mail, and of Arkle's granddam Greenogue Princess). Bought as a yearling by Harry Bonner on behalf of the flour millionaire J. V. Rank, he was sent to be broken to the young vet Bobby Power in County Cork. But Power was killed while mending a puncture on his car on the way to the Dublin Horse Show, and Rank's horses in Ireland were transferred in spring 1938 to Tom Dreaper, in whose hands Prince Regent learnt his jumping skills in the hunting field. A year later he was moved across to England to join Gwyn Evans, Rank's English trainer, but after Evans was himself killed, in a car crash, the horse found himself once more with Dreaper.

In terms of his impact on racing history it was Prince Regent's misfortune to live when he did, for very little steeplechasing took place in Britain during the war, and it was not until he was getting past his prime that he was able to display his talents on the larger stage across the Irish Sea.

Those talents were prodigious, though he started quietly. In his first season – 1939-40 – he ran in three bumper races, partnered in all three by his trainer, and won one. The following season he was unplaced in his debut chase, then won a hurdle at Phoenix Park and the Mickey Macardle Memorial Cup at Dundalk. In the 1941-2 season he won five of his seven races, a campaign crowned by victory in the Irish Grand National with 12st 7lb on his back, a performance which launched Prince Regent into the ranks of the great horses.

The magnificent Prince Regent with Tom Dreaper

The trouble was, with opportunities confined to Ireland, Prince Regent was for the moment confined to a more parochial greatness than would have been the case in peacetime, and was competing against many good horses who in normal circumstances would have been exported to England. The prize money was for the most part derisory. Prince Regent netted Mr Rank £745 when winning the Irish Grand National and £257 in the race before that, the Baldoyle Chase (the first occasion on which he was ridden by Tim Hyde). But his three other victories that season brought in two first prizes of £41 and one of £83!

By now the handicapper was taking no chances, and Prince Regent regularly had to shoulder huge weights. He won three races in the 1942-3 term, including a famous neck victory over Prince Blackthorn in the Baldoyle Chase, and in the Irish National only just failed to give thirty-three pounds to Golden Jack – on whom the handicapper was officially proclaimed to have been too lenient. Prince Regent was second in the 1944 Irish National, again carrying 12st 7lb, beaten a length by Knight's Crest, to whom he conceded three stone. His one chasing victory that season was in the Baldoyle Chase, which he won after a stirring duel over the last mile with Prince Blackthorn, who fell at the last. In December 1944 he took his revenge on Knight's Crest at Leopardstown, but after one more outing was sidelined by a warble and did not race for eight months.

By the start of his 1945-6 campaign the war was over and jump racing in Britain was slowly gathering momentum again. But Prince Regent was not far off eleven years old and time was running out for him to demonstrate his greatness in the big English chases.

Not that his Irish races gave any suspicion that his form was deteriorating. On his reappearance at Leopardstown in November 1945 he gave three stone to the 1940 Cheltenham Gold Cup winner Roman Hackle, and went under by a head. It was time to give him some experience of English fences (especially of the water jump, which did not exist in Ireland), and in December he made the trip to Wetherby for the Bradford Chase. He may have been Tom Dreaper's first runner in England but his fame had preceded him, and he started at 10-1 on, with his four rivals all on 20-1. The form book tells the story neatly: 'grand jmpr: made all: peckd at wtr: easd on flat'. He won by a cheeky half a length.

After a narrow defeat under 12st 7lb when third in the Baldoyle Chase, Prince Regent returned to England for the Gold Cup – accompanied, as befits a superstar, by his personal bodyguard. A record crowd of 35,000 turned out to see him and having marvelled in the paddock at his superbly built seventeen-hand physique backed him down to 7-4 on favourite. He justified the odds readily enough, taking the lead after the fifth fence and coming away from Poor Flame at the last to win by five lengths. But old age was beginning to make its presence felt, and Tim Hyde had to report to Tom Dreaper on dismounting: 'It took me a moment or two to beat that fellow today.' It was a poor Gold Cup field, and Prince Regent was clearly on the wane.

Three weeks later Prince Regent carried 12st 5lb and started 3-1 favourite in the first post-war Grand National. Taking up the running at Valentine's Brook second time round, he suffered from the attentions of loose horses but was still in the lead at the last fence. Then on the run-in the weight took its toll and he was passed by Lovely Cottage and by Jack Finlay, finishing third, seven lengths behind the winner. It was a stupendous effort.

In the following year's National, Prince Regent carried 12st 7lb. He again started favourite (at 8-1) and again ran heroically to come fourth behind Caughoo. By then he had won at Liverpool, taking the Champion Chase at 6-1 on in November 1946, and he added the Becher Chase in November 1947. But his third run in the National itself in 1948 at the age of thirteen could produce no fairytale: he was carried out by a loose horse at the fence after Becher's on the second circuit and pulled up.

There followed an attempt to retire the horse, but he did not take idleness well and was returned to training with Fred Horris in England. He won at Cheltenham and Lingfield in the 1948-9 season, and was third to Wot No Sun and Roimond in the valuable Emblem Chase at Manchester in November 1949. Behind him in fourth place and receiving a pound from the fourteen-year-old Irish horse was the eight-year-old Freebooter, who would win the next Grand National. Prince Regent's final race came the following month, when he fell in a three-runner chase at Lingfield Park.

The unfortunate timing of his birth and the consequent restriction of his racing to Ireland until he was creeping past his best have made Prince Regent difficult to place exactly in the ranks of the best chasers, but there is no denying him his place among the greats.

Down in Churchtown, County Cork, they still talk of how the bonfires burnt and the drink flowed the night **Cottage Rake** won his first Cheltenham Gold Cup, of how Vincent O'Brien was carried shoulder-high around the village, and of how O'Brien, owner Frank Vickerman and Cottage Rake's breeder Dr Otto Vaughan dispensed sweets to the schoolchildren.

In contrast to the big, strong Prince Regent, Cottage Rake – by the great Irish sire Cottage – was a light-framed horse who carried his head high and exhibited much more quality than the typical chaser of the time. Not that he was simply a chaser. In a versatile career he won three races on the Flat – including the Irish Cesarewitch at The Curragh in 1947 – as well as one hurdle and twelve steeplechases, notably, of course, three consecutive Cheltenham Gold Cups.

Cottage Rake was bred by Dr Vaughan of Mallow, spent much of his youth turned out on a bog, and was sent at the age of five to a young Churchtown trainer named Vincent O'Brien. The gelding somewhat unexpectedly won a maiden hurdle at Limerick in

December 1945 and then – more predictably – a bumper at Leopardstown the following February, after which he became a sought-after property. After various purchases failed to go through on account of doubts about the horse's wind, Cottage Rake was sold to O'Brien's first patron, the wool merchant Frank Vickerman.

His first run over fences was at Leopardstown on 26 December 1946 in the Carrickmines Chase, then an important novice event, and here he was ridden for the first time by the jockey with whose name he will for ever be associated, Aubrey Brabazon. He won by twenty lengths at 7-4 on, and proceeded to land his next two chases before running third in the Champion Novice Chase at Naas.

Having picked up the Irish Cesarewitch in November 1947, Cottage Rake returned to jumping with a stylish victory at Leopardstown just after Christmas, and the 1948 Gold Cup looked a real possibility. He fell in his preliminary race, the Leopardstown Chase, and although he was recognised in Ireland as a horse of exceptional promise, he started at Cheltenham at 10-1. By the last ditch Cottage Rake and Happy Home had drawn clear, with Martin Molony on Happy Home trying to bustle up his less experienced rival. Happy Home held the advantage at the last but Brabazon was not to be panicked, and he pulled Cottage Rake together and set off up the hill in pursuit of the leader. Cottage Rake caught Happy Home on the run-in and drew away to win by a length and a half. He followed this with a second in the Irish Grand National carrying 12st 7lb, and that was enough for the season.

The following autumn he ran in four chases (plus the Irish Cesarewitch again, in which he was unplaced), winning at Limerick Junction before crossing to England to land the Emblem Chase at Manchester, beating Silver Fame by a neck, and the King George VI Chase at Kempton, in which he defeated another of Lord Bicester's fine chasers in Roimond.

He did not run again before the Gold Cup, which in 1949 was moved to April after frost had caused the postponement of the race in March. Cottage Rake started 6-4 on favourite to beat five rivals, and was again taken on from the last open ditch. This time the challenger was Cool Customer, who led over the last, but again Brabazon was able to conjure a mighty run up the Cheltenham hill from Cottage Rake, and to Irish cheers which foretold the rapture which would greet Arkle fifteen years later, the O'Brien horse forged into the lead and won by two lengths.

Another King George was now top of the agenda, but this time Cottage Rake had to give best to yet another of the great Lord Bicester chasers, Finnure, to whom he was conceding eleven pounds. Dick Francis had ridden Roimond to defeat behind Cottage Rake a year earlier, and now had the ride on Finnure:

Coming second to him had made me all too painfully aware of the winning tactics usually adopted by Cottage Rake's great Irish jockey, Aubrey Brabazon, and consequently I gave a lot of thought to the tactics I planned to adopt. These crystallized in essence as keeping closely within touch of Cottage Rake and not letting him get unexpectedly into an accelerating lead.

The tactics worked like a dream, and

As we were approaching the last fence of all, I realized my mount was meeting it absolutely in his stride. I asked him for a major effort and this he gave, and with the momentum with which we were travelling, we passed Cottage Rake in mid-air and landed full of running about three-quarters of a length to the good. From that point on the battle really commenced, the two horses giving their all and galloping away from the opposition. Finnure and I came out on top and finished a neck in front of Cottage Rake at the post.

It was the first time that the Rake had been beaten on British soil.

Cottage Rake was brought down in the Leopardstown Chase, and then went to Cheltenham for a third Gold Cup. Again there were six runners, and again Cottage Rake went off an odds-on favourite – this time at 6-5 on. Finnure was 5-4, with the next horse 28-1. If ever there was a two-horse race, this was it.

The field set off at such a funereal pace that Irish commentator Michael O'Hehir described it on air as 'a slow bicycle race'. Martin Molony, riding Finnure, kept close behind Cottage Rake, hoping to repeat the Dick Francis tactics which had filched the King George, but Aubrey Brabazon stole the tactical advantage at the top of the hill on the second circuit by suddenly asking Cottage Rake to quicken his pace. Within seconds he was half a dozen lengths clear, beyond the reach of Finnure's attempts to peg him back. Cottage Rake won by ten lengths. Brabazon had ridden a brilliant tactical race – no wonder photographs of the Rake popping over the last show his jockey grinning.

Brabazon had also won the Champion Hurdle at the meeting on Hatton's Grace. It had been some week for him, but it ended on a downbeat. Riding the 7-1 on favourite Tsaoko in a novices' hurdle at Hurst Park on the Saturday, the jockey had dropped his hands close home and been caught on the line by Tory II, which incurred the wrath of the stewards. A newspaper headed the story, 'Caught Napping' – at which Vincent O'Brien wryly noted: 'Poor Aubrey, it was the only sleep he had during the week!'

After failing again to give lumps of weight away in the Irish Grand National, Cottage

Cottage Rake (Aubrey Brabazon) being led out by his trainer Vincent O'Brien before the 1948 King George VI Chase at Kempton Park

Rake was retired for the season, and was afflicted by a freak accident. He was let out in a field every day with a donkey for a companion, and one day the cattle who spent the night in that field were inadvertently left in when horse and donkey took the air. The donkey wandered in among the cattle and Cottage Rake, having lost sight of his friend, panicked. He tore around the field looking for his companion, got too close to the corner, and damaged a tendon.

He was never the same horse again, and never won another race. He ran three times – all unplaced – in the 1950-1 season and just once the following term. He was then moved to the stable of Gerald Balding in England, for whom he ran four times, still without success. His swansong came in a £204 chase at Wolverhampton in December 1953, just three weeks short of his fifteenth birthday. His rider that day was Dick Francis, who had so carefully plotted his defeat in the King George, but his memory is inextricably linked with Aubrey Brabazon – in the record books and in one of the most joyous of Irish racing rhymes:

Aubrey's up, the money's down
The frightened bookies quake
Come on me lads and give a cheer
Begod, 'tis Cottage Rake!

★　★　★

'Begod, 'tis **Flyingbolt!**' was an exclamation more likely to be uttered in sheer terror than in elation, for this inmate of Tom Dreaper's yard was almost as famous for his bad temper and general hostility to the human race as for his exploits on the track.

His achievements were considerable, and at his peak he was officially handicapped just two pounds below Arkle. So it is strange that this exceptional and highly versatile horse tends to be left out of discussions about who were the real champions, recently revived by supporters of Desert Orchid. While he should be another of the flag-bearers of the reputation of Ireland in racing, Flyingbolt is to some extent the Forgotten Great of post-war jumping.

By the Irish-bred 1946 Derby winner Airborne, Flyingbolt was temperamentally as different as could be from his distinguished contemporary Arkle. A huge, flashy chestnut with a large white blaze down his nose, he was, not to mince words, a brute. Whereas children could wander into Arkle's box in complete safety, nobody was safe with Flyingbolt. 'He would eat you' is the common reminiscence of those closest to him.

The career of Flyingbolt – the first horse his owner Mrs T. G. Wilkinson had in training – divides into two distinct phases.

For his first three seasons he was practically unbeatable. After educational runs in a Flat race at Leopardstown in May 1963 and a bumper at Navan and another Flat race at Leopardstown later that year, he won four consecutive races over hurdles, including the

Scalp Hurdle at Leopardstown in February 1964 (Arkle won the following race as his final preparation for the famous Gold Cup
showdown with Mill House) and the first division of the Gloucestershire Hurdle at the big Cheltenham meeting. Switched to
fences, he went through the next term unbeaten, winning three
chases at Leopardstown before returning to Cheltenham in March
1965 to win the two-mile Cotswold Chase. He then rounded off the
season with a victory at Fairyhouse.

Flyingbolt was now six, and had not been beaten since his first
race. If he had not fired the public imagination in the way that
Arkle had by the same stage of his career, that is partly because he
had no Mill House to raise his profile. But the 1965-6 season really
proclaimed his greatness. After a warm-up hurdle at Phoenix Park
he won four important races in a row – the Carey's Cottage Chase
at Gowran Park, the Black and White Gold Cup at Ascot, the
Massey-Ferguson Gold Cup at Cheltenham and the Thyestes Chase
at Gowran Park – before heading again for the big National Hunt
meeting at Cheltenham.

Flyingbolt had so much speed that an ambitious plan was laid to
run him in the Champion Hurdle, and Pat Taaffe was keen that he
should arrive at that race completely fresh. But the Two Mile
Champion Chase (in those days run the day before the Champion
Hurdle) was clearly at his mercy, and Tom Dreaper – assuring
Taaffe that 'a bird in the hand is worth two in the bush' – adopted
the bold strategy of going for both races.

Flyingbolt duly won the Two Mile Champion Chase in a canter
from Flash Bulb and Flying Wild, and the following day lined up
against the cream of the hurdlers. He was the all-rounder up
against the specialists, but heavy support in the betting ring sent
him off favourite at 15-8. Wary of mixing it with the expert
hurdlers, Pat Taaffe kept him on the outside of the field, joining
issue with the leaders Tamerosia and Kirriemuir at halfway. Then
just when Flyingbolt should have stepped up the pace to capitalise
on his stamina, he made a comprehensive mess of the fourth last
flight of hurdles and lost his momentum. He recovered but the
initiative was lost, and though he had regained the lead by the
second last, he was passed by the second favourite Salmon Spray
and on the run-in by Sempervivum. Flyingbolt was third, beaten

three lengths and three quarters of a length.

Though defeated in the Champion Hurdle, Flyingbolt's performances on consecutive days at the 1966 National Hunt meeting were
a remarkable feat.

He returned to Ireland, and to steeplechasing, and carried 12st
7lb to victory in the Irish Grand National, giving Height O'Fashion
forty pounds and a two-length beating. In her previous race Height
O'Fashion, a tough and consistent mare, had received forty-two
pounds from Arkle and been beaten a neck, so a line through her
put the two great Dreaper horses very close together. In the next
handicap for which both were entered, Arkle was allotted 12st 7lb,
Flyingbolt 12st 5lb.

After the Irish Grand National, Flyingbolt went into decline, and
he only won one more race. Beset by illness and training prob-
lems, he never recaptured his true form, and he was sent to
England to be trained by Ken Oliver (for whom he was second to
Titus Oates in the 1969 King George VI Chase) and then by Roddy
Armytage. His last race was the Topham Trophy at Liverpool in
April 1971, where he fell at the fourteenth fence.

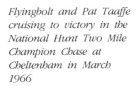

Flyingbolt and Pat Taaffe
cruising to victory in the
National Hunt Two Mile
Champion Chase at
Cheltenham in March
1966

Given that Flyingbolt's racing career never reached a plateau of achievement comparable with Arkle's, and that he did not get into the habit of winning the races which matter most to racing enthusiasts, it is not surprising that he failed to excite any of the rapture which surrounded his stable-companion. But at his best he was a superb horse, and the question which really intrigues is how those closest to him felt he compared with his illustrious contemporary.

Tom Dreaper tried working them together just once, with Pat Taaffe on Arkle and Paddy Woods on Flyingbolt. Taaffe has related how the two horses took each other on over four schooling fences 'while Paddy and I just held on to them for dear life and waited for the fires to die down'. They did not work together again.

Reflecting on the two horses years later, Pat Taaffe was in no doubt what would have been the outcome had they ever raced against each other: 'Flyingbolt was a front runner. Arkle would have been able to sit on his tail and beat him for speed.'

Flyingbolt may have recorded form of the highest order – he was the only horse apart from Arkle ever to receive a *Timeform* rating of over 200, being assessed at 210 after the Irish Grand National – but he was not, as was Arkle, easy to love. You kept your distance from Flyingbolt, physically and emotionally.

Apart from Dawn Run, to whose unique record we will turn shortly, two Irish Champion Hurdlers in the post-war period deserve particular mention.

Hatton's Grace was the first horse to win the Champion Hurdle three times, which he did in 1949, 1950 and 1951. Bred in Tipperary, he was initially sold at Goffs for just 18 guineas and eventually was purchased by Mrs Moya Keogh, who sent him to Vincent O'Brien in the summer of 1948. A small and unprepossessing gelding – later to be dubbed by Michael O'Hehir 'the ugly duckling of the parade ring' – Hatton's Grace had won two bumpers and three hurdles from twenty-three starts under the care of Barney Nugent before arriving at O'Brien's yard at Churchtown.

His first Champion Hurdle in 1949 was only his third run for

Vincent O'Brien, and, ridden by Aubrey Brabazon, he started at 100-7. National Spirit, who had won the race for the previous two years, was 5-4 favourite, but he could only manage fourth as Hatton's Grace, having taken up the running approaching the third last flight, charged up the hill to win by six lengths.

Less than a month later the versatile Hatton's Grace was again running on the Flat, ridden by Morny Wing to land the Irish Lincolnshire over one mile at The Curragh. Come November 1949 and he was back at The Curragh to take the Irish Cesarewitch (two miles), then two hurdles at Leopardstown before returning to Cheltenham to defend his crown.

National Spirit was back again, still immensely popular with the home crowd and still in good form, having won all his four races that season. He had a half-length lead over Hatton's Grace at the final flight, with Speciality and Harlech in close attendance, but National Spirit overjumped and threw the initiative to the Irish horse, who seized it and ran on gamely to win by one and a half lengths.

In November 1951 Hatton's Grace again won the Irish Cesarewitch, ridden this time by Martin Molony, and the following spring

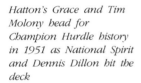

Hatton's Grace and Tim Molony head for Champion Hurdle history in 1951 as National Spirit and Dennis Dillon hit the deck

was back at Cheltenham as an eleven-year-old to bid for that un-precedented third Champion Hurdle. So was National Spirit, but neither started favourite. That honour went to the uninspiringly named Average, ridden by Aubrey Brabazon. Tim Molony rode Hatton's Grace, and again the ugly duckling came to the last half a length behind National Spirit: whichever way this went, there would be a triple Champion Hurdler. But National Spirit, looking to seal the outcome with a huge leap, slipped on landing and rolled over, leaving Hatton's Grace to record a simple victory.

The following year Hatton's Grace and National Spirit both re-turned for the Champion, but were unplaced behind a new star, Sir Ken.

At the age of twelve, the indefatigable Hatton's Grace took up steeplechasing, winning his final race at Leopardstown soon after his thirteenth birthday. He was then retired to Vincent O'Brien's new yard at Ballydoyle, where he was kept busy leading the younger horses in their work.

Hatton's Grace may not have been the most handsome horse ever to carry the Irish flag in the big English races, but he was cer-tainly one of the most charismatic, and he enjoyed a huge popular following in his home country. As Aubrey Brabazon said: 'It was probably because he was such a miserable and scraggy-looking devil that they took him to their hearts.'

The other great hurdler to touch Irish hearts was **Monksfield**, winner of the Champion Hurdle in 1978 and 1979 and runner-up in 1977 and 1980.

The story of Monksfield – very well told in Jonathan Powell's book about him – is an engaging one. His dam Regina was very well bred but of little account on the racecourse and unpromising as a broodmare. Sent by her owner Peter Ryan to the Coolmore stallion Gala Performance, who stood at £300, she produced a bay colt foal whose action in his faster paces as he matured was deemed severely deficient: he displayed a 'winding' motion in his forelegs. As a yearling he attracted no interest at Goffs sales, but the following year the diminutive two-year-old was sold for 740 guineas to a then obscure young trainer named Des McDonogh: 'I loved that head, that *fabulous* head, the instant I saw it.' Based at Billywood Stud, on the borders of County Meath and County Cavan, McDonogh had been training for less than two years. The horse then known as 'Smarty' was sold on for £1,125 to Dr Michael Mangan, a Galway-born radiologist in a Newfoundland hospital.

Monksfield, as the colt was named, won his first race, a maiden plate at Punchestown in October 1974, at odds of 25-1. Dr Mangan, at work in Newfoundland, had asked his mother-in-law in Ireland to put £10 on the horse for him on the Tote. She forgot, and had to report that the Tote odds on the winner had been 647-1 . . .

Third in the Irish Cesarewitch as a three-year-old in 1975, Monksfield's attentions were then switched to hurdling. He won four races during his juvenile season and, ridden by Tommy Kinane, was beaten only one and a half lengths by Peterhof in the 1976 Daily Express Triumph Hurdle at Cheltenham after meeting serious interference. The following month he won an apprentice race at Naas ridden by Tommy Kinane's sixteen-year-old son Michael.

His second jumping season was geared towards the Champion

Monksfield (Dessie Hughes, left) and Sea Pigeon (Jonjo O'Neill) in a familiar situation – locked together at the final flight of the Champion Hurdle. This is 1979 – when Monksfield battled on to win for the second time

Hurdle, for which he started at 15-1. Upsides Night Nurse and just ahead of Dramatist at the last, he slithered through a bad patch of ground and made a costly mistake, but recovered well enough to chase Night Nurse doggedly up the run-in before giving best by two lengths. The following month he took on Night Nurse again in the Templegate Hurdle at Liverpool and the two produced one of the greatest jumping races of the modern era to run a dead heat.

Monksfield's campaign in the 1977-8 season was interrupted by a leg infection, but an encouraging run when third to Prominent King in the Erin Foods Champion Hurdle at Leopardstown in February set him up for the Champion Hurdle. Night Nurse was back to try for a third win, and started 3-1 favourite. Sea Pigeon was a 5-1 chance, Monksfield 11-2. Racing downhill towards the third last Night Nurse and Monksfield were matching strides, and Sea Pigeon was making his move from the rear. Then Night Nurse weakened, and it was left to Sea Pigeon to challenge going to the last, but Monksfield put in a tremendous leap and landed running. With that fabulous head almost scraping the ground, he ran on un-falteringly up the hill to win by two lengths. He was the first entire to win the Champion Hurdle since Saucy Kit in 1967, and the first winner that Des McDonogh had trained for ten months.

Monksfield again went on to Liverpool to win the Templegate Hurdle from Night Nurse, the concession of five pounds to the former champion no doubt accounting for his generous starting price of 9-4. He ended the season with a heroic effort in the Royal Doulton Handicap Hurdle at Haydock Park, going down by just three quarters of a length to Royal Gaye, to whom he was giving two stone.

By now a celebrity, Monksfield had public duties to perform in Ireland before he could settle down to his summer break, the most nerve-wracking being his appearance at the Moynalty steam threshing festival, where he led a procession of steam engines and threshing machines. Such was the price of fame.

Monksfield's third Champion Hurdle produced one of the great races of recent memory, but it was preceded by controversy. Tommy Kinane was replaced on the horse by Dessie Hughes – who had ridden him in both Templegate Hurdles – after Kinane's riding of Monksfield in the 1979 Erin Foods Champion Hurdle had attracted criticism. Then rumours flew around. The most bizarre was that Monksfield had been indulging in a bout of self-abuse in his box (surely not something a Catholic horse would do). More plausible gossip had the horse lame and a doubtful runner, and for good measure it was said that Sea Pigeon had been bursting blood vessels and was not properly fit.

Both horses gave the lie to the rumours with a memorable race. For the second year in succession they hurtled towards the last flight together, but this time Sea Pigeon – ridden by Jonjo O'Neill – looked to be going much the better. They took off and landed in unison, then Sea Pigeon grabbed a narrow lead and made for the winning post. But Monksfield would not be denied. Pointing his nose to the turf like some equine truffle hound, he clawed his way back and in one of the finest finishes ever seen at Cheltenham stuck his head in front close home to win by three quarters of a length.

As usual Monksfield went on to Liverpool, winning what had by then become the Colt Sigma Hurdle from Kybo after Sea Pigeon had fallen at the last. He then won the Welsh Champion Hurdle at Chepstow and again failed gallantly in the Royal Doulton at Haydock, beaten two lengths by Beacon Light, to whom he was conceding thirteen pounds, in unsuitably soft going.

Monksfield was voted the National Hunt Racehorse of the Year in 1979: the only other Irish-trained jumper to have won the award by that time was Arkle.

He ran in the Champion Hurdle in 1980 and for the third year in a row came to the last with Sea Pigeon, but this time had to admit defeat by seven lengths. It was the first time in six races that Sea Pigeon had beaten his great rival, and only Persian War had finished first or second in four consecutive Champion Hurdles. Monksfield was then beaten by Pollardstown at Liverpool, won an amateur riders' race at Down Royal and on his last run finished down the field in the Royal Doulton Handicap – the only time in thirteen races in Great Britain that he failed to finish in the first two. He was retired to the Anngrove Stud in County Laois, where he died in 1989.

Monksfield ran in seventy-six races, winning five on the Flat and fourteen over timber. He was one of the great hurdlers, and a

One future racehorse who'll never be without a prayer: a foal and admirers at the Coolmore Stud

The great Tom Dreaper (top left) *and his most famous charge at the height of his powers:* (above) *Pat Taaffe and Arkle lead David Nicholson and Mill House on the first circuit of the Gallaher Gold Cup at Sandown Park in 1965, and* (left) *an unperturbed Arkle in the unsaddling enclosure*

The bedlam in the
Cheltenham unsaddling
enclosure on 13 March
1986 after Dawn Run had
become the only horse ever
to win the Cheltenham Gold
Cup and the Champion
Hurdle. Owner Mrs
Charmian Hill – whose
outfit matches jockey Jonjo
O'Neill's – and her son
Oliver lead the celebrations

Vincent O'Brien, Master of Ballydoyle. Right: *at The Curragh on Irish Derby Day 1991 with Lester Piggott (in the colours of Classic Thoroughbreds) and Robert Sangster.* Below: *Piggott in the same colours gets Royal Academy up to win the Breeders' Cup Mile at Belmont Park in October 1990*

Above: *the gallops at Ballydoyle.* Left: *Alleged and Lester Piggott (in the Robert Sangster colours) land the first of their two Prix de l'Arc de Triomphe, beating Balmerino in 1977*

Opposite: *another big win in 1977 for the O'Brien/Sangster/Piggott combination: The Minstrel battles home from Hot Grove (Willie Carson) in the Derby, with Blushing Groom (Henri Samani) third*

Temples of Irish breeding. Top: *the statue of Be My Guest which greets visitors to Coolmore.* Above: *the Kildangan Stud*

The variety of racing in Ireland. Above: *the one-day-a-year fixture on the sands at Laytown, and* (right) *the Boggeragh Mountains provide a glorious backdrop for a hurdle race at Mallow*

glowing tribute to the toughness and endurance of the Irish race-horse. The abiding memory of his racing career is of dogged, never-say-die determination. Head thrust down and every sinew pumping him home up the Cheltenham hill, his name will remain synonymous with courage in racing. As *Timeform* recorded: 'He was one of the gamest racehorses we ever set eyes on.'

As the only horse ever to win the Champion Hurdle and the Cheltenham Gold Cup, **Dawn Run** has not just an honoured but a unique place in racing history, and her death at the age of eight in the Grande Course de Haies at Auteuil in June 1986 robbed the sport of one of its most popular competitors.

By the greatest Irish jumping sire Deep Run, Dawn Run was bought as a three-year-old for 5,800 guineas by Mrs Charmian Hill, among the most remarkable characters ever to tread the Irish racing stage. Mrs Hill began race riding after her family had grown up, and was over forty when she started out as a jockey in point-to-points. In 1974 she became the first woman in the British Isles to compete against men over hurdles, and in all rode eighteen winners before in June 1982 the Turf Club decided that at sixty-three she was too old to carry on riding. She did not take this decision well, but went out on a high note by riding the four-year-old Dawn Run to victory in a bumper at Tralee.

That was Dawn Run's third race – she had been ridden in all three by her owner – and first win. In her next two bumpers, both of which she won, she was partnered by Tom Mullins, son of the trainer Paddy Mullins to whom she had been sent by Mrs Hill. After one more educative bumper Dawn Run's sights were set on hurdling, and by the end of her first season over timber she had become a force to be reckoned with, winning five times (including the valuable Findus Beefburger Hurdle at Leopardstown and the BMW Champion Novices' Hurdle at Punchestown, and ridden in all five by Tom Mullins's brother Tony) and running second in two important events in England: the Sun Alliance Hurdle at the Cheltenham Festival (beaten by Sabin Du Loir) and the Sun Templegate Hurdle at Liverpool (narrowly beaten by the Champion Hurdler Gaye Brief). The latter race came the day after she had won the

Page Three Handicap Hurdle at Liverpool, and already Dawn Run was being recognised as a young hurdler of exceptional promise and toughness.

Her resilience and determination on the racecourse reflected her home personality. 'She was very bossy,' recalls Paddy Mullins: 'She'd have a go at you when you went into her stable. And on the gallops she had to be the boss – she didn't like anything to beat her.' That quality would stand her in good stead

Although she would surely make a chaser in due course, the focal point of Dawn Run's next season was to be the Champion Hurdle. With that target in mind Mrs Hill, who was not a lady to spare a jockey the benefit of her views if she thought he had not ridden the best possible race, left off the mare's regular partner Tony Mullins for her first big contest of the new term, the VAT Watkins Hurdle at Ascot, and engaged Jonjo O'Neill. Starting at 3-1 on, Dawn Run did not advertise her championship claims by barely scraping home from the unfancied Amarach.

But she catapulted herself back into the Champion Hurdle reckoning with a marvellous neck defeat of the reigning champion Gaye Brief in the Ladbroke Christmas Hurdle on Boxing Day, staying on up the straight with the utmost gameness and simply refusing to let Gaye Brief past. She then won the Wessel Cable Champion Hurdle at Leopardstown and in the absence of Gaye Brief, sidelined through injury, went to Cheltenham a hot favourite at 5-4 on. From the start of the 1983-4 season a five-pound weight concession was allowed to mares in British National Hunt races, and she needed the advantage which this gave her, scrambling home by three quarters of a length from Cima. But the less than impressive manner of her victory did not bother the legions of Irish supporters who had crammed Cheltenham, and in what in retrospect looked like a gentle warm-up for the pandemonium to come two years later, the first mare to win the Champion Hurdle since African Sister in 1939 was accorded a rousing reception in the winner's enclosure.

With Tony Mullins back in the saddle, Dawn Run sauntered to an easy victory in the Sandeman Aintree Hurdle at Liverpool and then had her attention fixed on a unique treble. Having won the Irish and English Champion Hurdles, she would go for the French

equivalent at Auteuil in June. After a preliminary Auteuil outing in the Prix la Barka, which she won, she was sent off a warm favourite for the Grande Course de Haies and put her rivals firmly in their place, leading all the way to win by six lengths.

Even before that victory she had been voted National Hunt Horse of the Year.

Dawn Run's later achievements and tragic end tend to deflect attention from her exploits as a hurdler. She may not have been the greatest ever seen, but she won thirteen of her twenty-one hurdle races, and her treble of international Champion Hurdles was an extraordinary feat.

Doubtless she would have dominated hurdling for a couple more years, but, says Paddy Mullins, 'Mrs Hill left me in no doubt that the Gold Cup was what she wanted', so that became the target.

She duly won her first race over the major obstacles, from Buck House and Dark Ivy at Navan in November 1984, but a leg injury then ruled her out for the rest of that season. She returned in December 1985 to beat much more experienced horses at

Oof! Never the most consistently elegant of jumpers, Dawn Run tests Jonjo O'Neill's adhesive qualities at the last flight before winning the 1984 Champion Hurdle

Punchestown and then landed the Sean P. Graham Chase at Leopardstown despite an almighty blunder at the last.

It was time to start getting serious about the 1986 Gold Cup, and experience of the undulations and uncompromising fences of Cheltenham was vital. So Dawn Run was sent across at the end of January for the Holsten Distributors Chase. Jumping somewhat extravagantly, she led her rivals until dislodging Tony Mullins at the open ditch at the top of the hill. Although her jockey swiftly remounted, the rest of the field were gone beyond recall, and so were his hopes of riding the mare in the Gold Cup.

Scarcely had he vaulted back into the saddle than the question of who should partner Dawn Run on her return to Cheltenham raged around the racecourse and in the press. 'Dare Mullins remain loyal?', boomed the front page of the *Sporting Life*, but it was a rhetorical question. The trainer would have to abide by the owner's decision, and no one was offering to lay odds about what that would be. The reaction to Dawn Run's misfortune in her first attempt at the Cheltenham fences, which after all was designed to be an educative outing, still rankles with Paddy Mullins – 'You'd think I'd done some dastardly deed' – and he remains convinced that Tony Mullins knew more about the horse and got more out of her than any other jockey. For the Cheltenham Gold Cup, however, Jonjo would have the mount.

Frost in Ireland cancelled Dawn Run's proposed preliminary race, so she went straight to Cheltenham with a big question mark hanging over her. The Gold Cup was only the fifth steeplechase of her life: would inexperience and indifferent jumping let her down?

Doubts or no doubts, she started favourite at 15-8 against most of the best chasers around, including the first three in the 1985 race – Forgive 'N Forget, Righthand Man and Earl's Brig. She led from the start but was soon joined by Run And Skip, and the distraction caused her to make a mistake at the third. These two went well clear of the rest of the field and were still dictating affairs when the pace was stepped up on the second circuit. Dawn Run dropped her hind legs in the water, and made another mistake five out, but the errors were not taking much out of her, and as the field came down the hill for the last time she was still in contention. Run And Skip touched down first at the third last but a gigantic leap from Dawn Run two out put her back in front, before being swamped by Wayward Lad and Forgive 'N Forget going to the last. As the three horses, all dog tired, headed up the hill Wayward Lad had the lead and seemed to be heading for the Gold Cup he so richly deserved, but he started to wander to the left, and this gave Jonjo O'Neill a glimpse of hope. Switching Dawn Run from the inside to the middle of the track, he conjured one final effort from her, and a few yards from the post she fought past Wayward Lad to win by a length. ('That was her nature,' remembers Paddy Mullins: 'She wouldn't give in.')

The race itself, stirring and memorable by any standards, was as nothing compared with the scenes which followed. As Dawn Run passed the winning post the Cheltenham sky became a cascade of hats, and the spectators – Irish and English alike – thundered their appreciation of a unique feat as Jonjo O'Neill, arm punched high in triumph, brought the mare back past the packed stands. A rapidly snowballing mass of people gathered in her wake as she was led up the horse-walk towards the unsaddling enclosure at the far end of Cheltenham's parade ring, then spilled and pushed and crammed into the enclosure as she was unsaddled.

Having weighed in, Jonjo O'Neill – as popular an Irishman as there is in racing and now at one of the high points of his career – was carried shoulder high. He in turn lifted the deposed Tony Mullins on to his shoulders, and Charmian Hill was likewise hoisted aloft. It was another great Cheltenham affirmation of Irish glory in racing, and as crack it took some beating.

Dawn Run returned to Ireland the following day, and to mark her triumphal progress back to the Mullins stable near Goresbridge, bonfires were lit that evening along the narrow road which leads to the yard from Royal Oak, just off the main route from Carlow to Kilkenny. She was a local heroine, but Dawn Run, like Arkle before her, now belonged to all Ireland.

After all the jubilation, the hangover was fierce. Dawn Run went to Liverpool for the Whitbread Gold Label Cup and came down at the first, giving O'Neill a terrible fall. Reunited with Tony Mullins, she then won a rousing £25,000 match against Buck House over two miles at Punchestown and headed back to France. She came second in the Prix la Barka, and again Mullins was jocked off: the

French jockey Michel Chirol was engaged to ride her in the Grande Course de Haies. At the fifth last hurdle she stood off too far, fell and broke her neck, dying instantly.

Dawn Run was only eight when she was killed, and could have been expected to enrapture her fans for a good few years. Instead we are left with the memory of another Irish jumper who illuminated the racing scene, and whose deeds spoke volumes about the quality of Irish horses and their compatriots who handle them. Dawn Run is appropriately commemorated by a bronze statue at the entrance to the Cheltenham parade ring. Charmian Hill died in January 1990.

Before we leave the leppers, a brief word about two other unforgettable jumpers.

L'Escargot is the only horse apart from Golden Miller to have won a Cheltenham Gold Cup and a Grand National, and one of only five horses to have won the Gold Cup more than once.

Bred in Mullingar, County Westmeath, L'Escargot was trained by Dan Moore for Raymond Guest, the American ambassador to Ireland, on whose behalf L'Escargot was purchased for 3,000 guineas. In a career which spanned ten seasons he ran sixty times, winning two races on the Flat, three hurdles (including a division of the Gloucestershire Hurdle at Cheltenham in 1968) and nine steeplechases. Nine may not seem a very big haul for one of the big names of chasing, but the nature of those victories proclaims L'Escargot's special place in the history of the Irish Turf.

In January 1970 he landed the valuable W. D. & H. O. Wills Premier Chase Final at Haydock well enough to indicate to connections that the 1970 Gold Cup might just be within his powers, but defeat in heavy ground at Leopardstown suggested to Moore that three miles was beyond him. Raymond Guest, however, insisted on running in the Gold Cup, and his judgement was vindicated. L'Escargot started at 33-1 but after the favourite Kinloch Brae

The blinkered head of L'Escargot (Tommy Carberry) looms alongside Red Rum (Brian Fletcher) at the last in the 1975 Grand National

had fallen at the third last tracked French Tan over the final fence and stayed on to win by one and a half lengths.

He did not win again until the following year's Gold Cup, for which he started 7-2 joint favourite with Into View and Leap Frog. Again the third last fence played its part in the race, Glencaraig Lady's fall there leaving L'Escargot in the lead from Leap Frog. In going described as 'very heavy', the horse whose stamina had at one time been doubted plugged on to win by ten lengths, with The Dikler a further fifteen lengths back in third.

Despite having won two Gold Cups, L'Escargot was by no means a popular hero. Possibly on account of his manner of racing with his ears set back, and with his handsome head shrouded in what became a very familiar pair of blue blinkers, he did not strike much of a chord in the public affections. But as his presence became a regular feature of the big occasions – he competed at the Cheltenham National Hunt Meeting seven times in eight years – so he grew in the public esteem.

For years Raymond Guest had been asking Dan Moore to buy him a horse to win the Grand National. 'You've got one,' Moore would reply. L'Escargot's record in the Grand National has a beautifully logical shape: three, two, one. In 1973 few paid much attention to his running on to take third place in the wake of the unforgettable duel between Crisp and Red Rum. In 1974 he improved to take the runner-up berth as Red Rum notched his second win, and then in 1975 he improved one place more.

Ridden as he had been in all his big races by Tommy Carberry, L'Escargot survived a terrible blunder at the seventh fence and reached the front rank on the run back from Valentine's on the second circuit. At the second last the race was between Red Rum and L'Escargot, but the big blinkered fellow was clearly going the better. 'Go on, Tommy – you'll win five minutes!', Brian Fletcher on Red Rum called across to Carberry, but L'Escargot's pilot was too wily an old hand to rush things, and he stayed with Red Rum until they had landed over the last. L'Escargot streaked clear and won, if not five minutes, by fifteen lengths.

And that should have been that. In the excitement of victory Guest announced that the horse would not run again but would be given to Dan Moore's wife Joan to hunt, on the understanding that he would not be asked to race. But the old horse did not take kindly to retirement, and in September 1975 he was sent to Listowel for the Kerry National, in which he was beaten a head by Black Mac. When the news reached Raymond Guest that L'Escargot had run, he insisted that the horse be dispatched to the USA – where he had won the Meadow Brook Chase at Belmont Park – for a more placid life, whether that suited him or no. L'Escargot died in Virginia at the age of twenty-one.

If L'Escargot did not quite trigger the public imagination – at least until he became a standing dish in the National – the same is partly true of **Captain Christy**, in many experts' estimation the closest we have seen to that elusive 'new Arkle'.

Captain Christy's overall record does not remotely stand comparison with Arkle's, though it is impressive enough. He won the Irish Sweeps Hurdle in 1972, the Cheltenham Gold Cup in 1974 and the King George VI Chase in 1974 and 1975 – in the latter King George producing one of the truly great individual performances of the modern era.

By the unfashionable sire Mon Capitaine, Captain Christy was bred in West Cork and purchased as a foal for 290 guineas; eventually he was sent to Pat Taaffe, by then training from his yard near Naas, and sold to the New Zealand entrepreneur Pat Samuel, in whose wife's colours the horse ran.

The most remarkable human connection of Captain Christy was his regular jockey Bobby Beasley. Having won the 1959 Gold Cup on Roddy Owen, the 1960 Champion Hurdle on Another Flash and the 1961 Grand National on Nicolaus Silver, in the late 1960s Beasley succumbed to the bottle after several bad falls and for a while was lost to racing. But with the stubborn support of a few friends, he gradually beat off alcoholism and hauled himself back. Having also shed much of the excess weight which the drink had larded on to him, he returned to race-riding at the end of 1970, and in February 1971 rode his comeback winner.

Pat Taaffe had kept faith with Bobby Beasley and now gave him the chance to ride his volatile new charge, Captain Christy. In December 1972 they won the important Sweeps Hurdle at Leopardstown, and the following spring came third to Comedy of Errors in the Champion Hurdle before going to Ayr to take the Scottish Champion Hurdle.

The next season Captain Christy, still a headstrong and unpredictable horse, went chasing. He won his first two in Ireland, then toppled over at the second last in the Black & White Whisky Gold Cup at Ascot when vying for the lead with Bula. After being placed in two good Irish hurdles, he returned to England for a big sponsored chase, the Wills Final at Haydock, and with the race completely at his mercy again blundered away his chance at the second last. Two more wins in Ireland, and then over to take his chance at Cheltenham.

Pendil was a very hot favourite for the 1974 Gold Cup following his narrow defeat by The Dikler in the previous year's race. Backers of Captain Christy saw him start at 7-1, a reasonable price given his chancy jumping.

But it was the jumping of the 100-1 outsider High Ken which altered the complexion of the race at the notorious downhill fence, the third last. High Ken was leading with Pendil behind him, but as they approached the fence The Dikler, Captain Christy and

Captain Christy (Bobby Coonan) in full flight in the 1974 King George VI Chase at Kempton Park

Game Spirit all made to move up towards the leader, and suddenly Richard Pitman on Pendil found himself trapped behind a notoriously risky jumper who was probably getting to the end of his tether. The worst happened. High Ken crumpled on landing and, to an almighty groan from the crowd, brought down Pendil.

This left The Dikler in the lead, but Captain Christy joined him at the second last. Although in front earlier than he wanted to be, Beasley had no option but to go for home. At the last he was about a length up, and Captain Christy chose this moment to produce his customary blunder, shooting Beasley up his neck. But the jockey was equal to the situation, gathered the horse together and made for the line, winning by five lengths.

The following month Captain Christy fell in the Irish Grand National and the next day won the Power Gold Cup. It was the last time that Beasley rode him.

Under his new jockey Bobby Coonan, Captain Christy turned in a tremendous performance to beat Pendil in the 1974 King George VI Chase, coming right away from his rival – who was in his element at Kempton – to win by eight lengths. He ran again in the Gold Cup but was pulled up in going so atrocious that the meeting was abandoned as soon as the main event had been run.

Captain Christy was second to April Seventh in the 1975 Whit-bread under 12st and the same year second in the Grand Steeplechase de Paris at Auteuil and fourth in the Colonial Cup at Camden, South Carolina.

But he reserved his greatest performance for his final race, the King George VI Chase on Boxing Day 1975. Ridden by young Gerry Newman after Coonan had been injured in a fall and starting 11-10 joint favourite with Bula, Captain Christy simply scorched round Kempton, meeting his fences with precision and jumping brilliantly – though he did land alarmingly steeply at the fourth from home. With Bula labouring in his wake, he screeched round the final bend and hammered up the straight to a rapturous reception from the crowd, who knew that they'd seen one of the great chasing performances – a view confirmed by the time of the race, four seconds inside the course record.

This was Captain Christy's day, and on his day he was a truly superb horse. In the opinion of his trainer: 'He was brilliant if he took it into his head to go, but he wasn't genuine.'

Signs of leg trouble were growing worrying, and Taaffe recommended a year's rest. Mrs Samuel disagreed, and took the horse away from Taaffe, sending him to Francis Flood. But he was never able to race again.

There are plenty of other Irish chasers and hurdlers who could claim a place in this chapter: any of Vincent O'Brien's three Grand National winners, especially Royal Tan; Fort Leney, a superb horse on his day and an underrated Gold Cup winner; Golden Cygnet, the brilliant novice hurdler tragically killed in 1978; two-mile chasers such as Fortria or Anaglog's Daughter. The range and variety of the Irish contribution to the star turns of National Hunt racing goes on and on, reaffirming the view of that nineteenth-century observer who thought Irish horses 'the highest and the steadiest leapers in the world'.

CHAPTER FOUR

ON THE FLAT

FLAT RACING is a much more international affair than jumping, and few of its equine participants can boast the through-and-through Irishness of the best jumpers. But there is nevertheless a recognition that some horses, were they to don national colours for their races, would be carrying the green, white and gold tricolour – and some years they plant that flag on the highest peaks of international racing. A true *annus mirabilis* for the Irish on the Flat, for instance, was 1958, when Hard Ridden won the Derby and Ballymoss and Gladness between them won the Coronation Cup, the Ascot Gold Cup, the Eclipse Stakes, the King George VI and Queen Elizabeth Stakes, the Goodwood Cup, the Ebor Handicap and the Prix de l'Arc de Triomphe.

Ballymoss, though owned by an American and ridden to many of his major victories by an Australian, had the Flat version of equine Irishness. Nijinsky, bred in Canada and owned by an American, had it.

Alleged, for all his brilliance on the racecourse, did not. By the

The first Irish-trained winner of an American Triple Crown race: Michael Kinane and Go And Go make racing history in the Belmont Stakes at Belmont Park, New York, in June 1990

time he was winning his Arcs in 1977 and 1978, Flat racing at the highest level had effectively transcended national boundaries. Alleged was trained in Ireland by Vincent O'Brien, but the colt represented the Sangster empire, then the major player in the burgeoning multi-million-dollar international bloodstock industry. Bred from the best American blood (and originally purchased by Sangster to race in California), Alleged was a player in a multinational game, and never quite caught the imagination as an 'Irish' horse.

The world of Flat racing is much larger and more complex than the jumping business, and most of the money which will buy success at the highest level is concentrated in a very few very well-known hands. So there is less opportunity for the sort of story which lies behind a Monksfield or a Dawn Run. And then, the top performers on the Flat tend to be around for such a short time – not time enough for any one of them to become, in the eyes of the racing public, a real and continuing champion of its country. But what is their country? Here we get back to the question of where a horse is trained. Generous was bred in Ireland, owned by an Arab prince and trained in England, but when he went to Paris for the Arc it was England he represented. National identities and loyalties become blurred.

The first Irish-trained horse to win the Derby was 'Boss' Croker's Orby in 1907. Over fifty years elapsed before the next, Hard Ridden, trained by Mick Rogers, in 1958. By 1984 another eight Irish-trained horses had been added to the Derby roll of honour, thanks mainly to Vincent O'Brien, who sent out six of them.

Vincent O'Brien was also responsible for **Ballymoss**, the first great Irish-trained horse in post-war European racing. Ballymoss did not win the Derby, but he was the first ever horse to win the St Leger for an Irish trainer, and went on to land four of the great European middle-distance races.

Ballymoss was bred at Naul, County Dublin, by Richard Ball (breeder of Reynoldstown), who had acquired his dam Indian Call for just 15 guineas, which proved to be something of a bargain:

apart from Ballymoss, the mare bred six other winners. Vincent O'Brien bought the yearling colt for 4,500 guineas on behalf of his patron John McShain, head of the American construction company which had built the Pentagon. (In the USA McShain raced under the name 'Barclay Stable' – hence his distinctive racing colours featuring the red 'B' on the back and front of the white jacket.)

The son of an Irish emigrant to Philadelphia, John McShain is a significant figure in the relationship between Ireland and the wider world of racing. Meeting O'Brien at Doncaster in 1955 led to more than his owning Ballymoss and Gladness: more significantly, in the long term, it led to O'Brien visiting Keeneland sales in Kentucky at McShain's invitation, thus introducing the trainer to the American bloodlines which were to prove such an important element in his success over the next thirty years.

Ballymoss gave little hint of the glories to come when winning just one small race from four outings as a two-year-old, though not for nothing has Vincent O'Brien gained a reputation as an unmatched judge of a horse's potential: reporting on that one win to McShain in America, he planted the idea that the colt should be aimed at the 1957 Derby.

At three, Ballymoss was unplaced in the Madrid Free Handicap but then caused a major surprise when winning the Trigo Stakes at Leopardstown at 20-1, with his stable-companion Gladness (to whom we will come shortly) the unplaced odds-on favourite. The fast going was a significant factor: Ballymoss loved it, Gladness hated it.

As part of the build-up to the Derby, Ballymoss took part in a mixed gallop with horses from the stables of Seamus McGrath and Paddy Prendergast, and won easily. A bruised foot then interrupted his preparation, but he was allowed to take his chance in the Classic. On form he had little prospect of beating the Two Thousand Guineas winner Crepello, and in the event he did not; but starting at 33-1, he ran a wonderful race under T. P. Burns to finish second, one and a half lengths behind the favourite.

He then took the Irish Derby in a canter at 9-4 on, though he was beaten in the Great Voltigeur Stakes at York on soft ground. Rain throughout the night before the St Leger saw his price being pushed out from 5-1 to 8-1, but he won well by a length from

Ballymoss (T. P. Burns) beating Court Harwell (Scobie Breasley) to become the first Irish-trained St Leger winner in September 1957

Court Harwell. He was subsequently unplaced in the Champion Stakes, when probably over the top for the season.

Ballymoss was not fully wound up when opening his four-year-old campaign with defeat by the Queen's Doutelle in the Ormonde Stakes at Chester, but then commenced his glorious quartet of the big middle-distance races, ridden in all four by Scobie Breasley. He comfortably beat Fric in the Coronation Cup and then hammered six rivals in the Eclipse Stakes: 'v. smoothly', said the form book. (That must have been some day's racing: two races before the Eclipse a two-year-old called Petite Etoile won the Star Stakes at 7-2.) One week later in the King George VI and Queen Elizabeth Stakes, Ballymoss was only marginally preferred in the betting to the Derby winner Hard Ridden, but took up the running a quarter of a mile out and quickened away to win comfortably from Almeria and Doutelle.

No Irish-trained horse had ever won the Prix de l'Arc de Triomphe when Ballymoss faced sixteen rivals at Longchamp on the first Sunday of October 1958, and a steady downpour from midday seemed to be lessening Ballymoss's chance of breaking the duck. Peter O'Sullevan, who had been asked by Vincent O'Brien to back the horse on his behalf, recalled the effect of the rain on the trainer's optimism:

The Bois de Boulogne circuit was no drier than the adjacent Seine. 'Any hope of laying off my bet?' inquired Vincent despairingly. There wasn't. Rae [Johnstone] paddled into the weighing room to advise Scobie to swim round the outside. He did so, and halfway up the Longchamp straight the winner of that season's Eclipse, Coronation Cup and King George VI and Queen Elizabeth Stakes accelerated like a power boat to give his barely recognizable mud-spattered partner his first victory in France.

Ballymoss had one more race, travelling to Laurel Park for the Washington International. The sharp track was all against him, and in a notoriously rough race he could finish only third. His career winnings of £107,165 passed Tulyar's British record, but his real achievement was to put Ireland in the front rank of world Flat racing. And, like Arkle, in 1981 Ballymoss was accorded the compliment of being depicted on an Irish postage stamp.

The career of Ballymoss is often bracketed with that of his stable-companion, the great mare **Gladness**. A year older than Ballymoss, the English-bred Gladness ran once at two (unplaced) and once at three, winning a maiden race at Manchester and landing, in O'Brien's words, 'a substantial gamble'. At four she was given 10st for the Irish Lincolnshire at The Curragh – automatic top weight as she had not run enough times to be handicapped – and came second at 25-1. She ran unplaced in the Trigo Stakes (the only time she ever raced against Ballymoss) and in the summer of 1957 was sold to John McShain, in whose colours she won the Sunninghill Park Stakes at Ascot and the Leinster Handicap at The Curragh before running unplaced behind Oroso in the Arc. She ended the season by winning the Champion Stakes at The Curragh.

Gladness carried the massive weight of 10st 10lb in the 1958 Irish Lincolnshire and unsurprisingly finished unplaced. She then went to France for the Prix du Cadran and was beaten a length by Scot II, with whom she started joint favourite for the Ascot Gold Cup. Here, ridden for the first time by Lester Piggott, she took her revenge. Second into the short Ascot straight, she took up the running a quarter of a mile out to win by a hard-fought length from Hornbeam. Scot II was fourth. She went on to take the Goodwood Cup, and then produced what for many people was one of the finest handicap performances of all time when lugging 9st 7lb to a

six-length victory over Woodside Terrace – who received twenty-nine pounds – in the Ebor Handicap at York.

Kept in training as a six-year-old, Gladness won one race at Phoenix Park and was unplaced in the Prix du Cadran before lining up as second favourite for the King George at Ascot. She ran her usual game race and set sail for home at the two-furlong pole, but had no answer to the devastating finish of Alcide and went down by two lengths. That was her last race.

Understandably John McShain was keen to mate his great horse Ballymoss with his great mare Gladness, and the best of their offspring was Bally Joy, who won three races and came third in the Hardwicke Stakes, while Merry Mate won the Irish Oaks in 1966. The finest horse sired by Ballymoss was Royal Palace, winner like his sire of the Coronation Cup, Eclipse and King George, as well as the Two Thousand Guineas and Derby.

Ballymoss was also the sire of a filly named Feemoss, who was to make her mark as the dam of **Levmoss**, in 1969 the second Irish-trained winner of the Prix de l'Arc de Triomphe.

Surrounded as he is in the record books by the famous horses trained by O'Brien and Prendergast, Levmoss has had something of a rum deal from history. But he was one of the finest horses

Gladness (Lester Piggott) wins the 1958 Ebor Handicap at York by six lengths

trained in Ireland this century, and deserves his position in the exhibition cases at Leopardstown racecourse celebrating the Irish in racing.

Levmoss was trained by Seamus McGrath, who had also trained his sire Le Levanstell, and raced just twice at two, winning once. At three he progressed to the verge of the highest class, running third in the Prix Royal-Oak and winning three races, notably the Oxfordshire Stakes at Newbury, in which he beat Canterbury (who went on to be beaten a short head by Ribero in the St Leger) and the great filly Park Top. That race was over one mile five furlongs, and the feeling that Levmoss was essentially a stayer was bolstered when he won the two-mile Leopardstown November Handicap carrying 9st 4lb.

In March 1969 he was unplaced in the Gladness Stakes at The Curragh over one mile, and third in April behind Zamazaan in the Prix Jean Prat at Longchamp over nearly twice that distance. In May he returned to Longchamp for the Prix du Cadran, at two and a half miles France's top staying race, and held off the late runs of Zamazaan and Samos III by a neck and a head. This put him right into the reckoning for the Ascot Gold Cup, for which he started favourite: he took up the running in the straight and won easily by four lengths from Torpid, in the process becoming the first horse

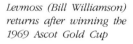

Levmoss (Bill Williamson) returns after winning the 1969 Ascot Gold Cup

since Arbar in 1948 to win the Prix du Cadran and the Ascot Gold Cup in the same year.

By this point Levmoss was clearly stamped as a stayer of the highest class, a view confirmed when he won a fourteen-furlong handicap at The Curragh under the crushing burden of 10st 10lb. It was then on to Longchamp for the Arc. The field he faced was a formidable one: it included Park Top, winner of the Coronation Cup and the King George, the first three in the Derby (Blakeney, Shoemaker and Prince Regent – not to be confused with Tom Dreaper's chaser!), the first two in the Irish Sweeps Derby (Prince Regent and Ribofilio), the first two in the French Oaks and Prix Vermeille, and the winners of the Italian Derby and the Grand Prix de Paris. In such company it was no surprise that Levmoss, ridden by Bill 'Weary Willie' Williamson, started at a pari-mutuel price of 52-1. (It is interesting to note that Gold River, in 1981 the next Prix du Cadran winner to land the Arc, started at almost identical odds.)

Riding Levmoss for the stamina which he knew the horse to have in abundance, Williamson took up the running at the entrance to the straight and readily held off challenge after challenge. Park Top, on whom Lester Piggott had been forced wide in order to find a clear run, came swooping up the outside in the final furlong but the post arrived in time for Levmoss, who won by three quarters of a length without Williamson having to go for his whip. The time for the race was a new course record.

There has been a tendency for the 1969 Arc to be remembered as a race lost by Park Top – Piggott received almost as much criticism over his ride as he would the following year on Nijinsky – but none the less Levmoss was a worthy winner, and a wonderful advertisement for Ireland and Irish breeding at the highest level of European racing. The colt retired after the Arc, and stood at the McGraths' Brownstown Stud until 1976 before being exported to France, where he died the following year. His full brother Le Moss won the stayers' treble of Ascot Gold Cup, Goodwood Cup and Doncaster Cup in 1979 and 1980.

If 1969 was the year of Levmoss, the years immediately before and after belonged to two of the legendary Vincent O'Brien colts whose exploits did so much to solidify the status of Ireland in international racing.

In his breeding, by Sir Gaylord out of Attica, **Sir Ivor** was American through and through. Having fetched $42,000 at the July 1966 Keeneland sales, he was sent by owner Raymond Guest to be trained at Ballydoyle and won three of his four starts as a two-year-old, notably the National Stakes at The Curragh and the Grand Criterium at Longchamp.

He was then sent to Italy for a winter holiday to escape the worst of the Irish climate, and the O'Brien enterprise yet again paid off. After winning at Ascot on his first appearance as a three-year-old, he faced the brilliant Petingo in the Two Thousand Guineas and showed what was to become his hallmark, a blazing moment of speed to go clear in the closing stages.

Despite predictable doubts about the staying power of a horse with such acceleration, Sir Ivor started 5-4 on favourite for the Derby. The depths of his stamina looked like being plumbed when Connaught set sail for home in the straight and showed no signs of flagging, but once Lester Piggott asked Sir Ivor for his burst the effect was deadly. In what Tony Morris described as 'the most devastating change of pace ever seen in the closing stages of a twelve-furlong classic', Sir Ivor had sprinted clear to win by one and a half lengths.

He seemed invincible, but he lost his next four races. Ribero outstayed him in the Irish Derby. Royal Palace and Taj Dewan got first run on him in a famous finish to the Eclipse. He was less than fully tuned up when beaten by Prince Sao in the Prix Henry Delamarre, and then returned to his top form in the Arc, only to find Vaguely Noble three lengths too good.

Sir Ivor picked up the winning thread again in the Champion Stakes at Newmarket over ten furlongs – almost certainly his best distance – and then went to Laurel Park for the Washington International. This proved a controversial race, with Piggott producing Sir Ivor from seemingly insurmountable difficulties in running to take the lead shortly before the wire and win by three quarters of a length. In Europe the jockey would probably have been applauded for riding a brilliantly timed race, but most of the

American press saw things differently, berating Piggott for nearly losing a race he should have won easily – and which, in Sir Ivor's terms, he *did* win easily.

Sir Ivor did not run again. To the alarm of fans of Royal Palace, he was voted Horse of the Year for 1968.

With Sir Ivor we see the notion of the 'Irish' horse on the Flat crumbling. American-bred and American-owned, ridden in most of his big races by an Englishman, he was one of the first who competed under racing's United Nations flag. But there was a boost to the Irish bloodstock industry when it was announced that for the first two years of his stallion career he would stand at the Ballygoran Stud in Maynooth, County Kildare. While there – then the most highly priced stallion ever to stand in Ireland – he sired Cavo Doro, bred by Lester Piggott and ridden by him when runner-up to Morston in the 1973 Derby. In his second crop he produced Sir Tristram, who was sent to New Zealand and became the most influential sire in the southern hemisphere. After his two seasons at the Ballygoran Stud, Sir Ivor was sent to the Claiborne Farm in Kentucky.

The 1968 Derby: Lester Piggott produces Sir Ivor (left) to fly past Sandy Barclay on Connaught

At the time Sir Ivor began his duties in America in 1971, Claiborne had just taken possession of an even more famous horse, and one whose name has remained synonymous with racing brilliance – **Nijinsky**.

Indisputably a great racehorse, Nijinsky's particular contribution to the place of Ireland in the racing world is that he was instrumental in attracting Vincent O'Brien to the Northern Dancer blood – which after Nijinsky would bring to Ballydoyle such horses as Be My Guest, The Minstrel, Try My Best, Storm Bird, Lomond, El Gran Senor and Sadler's Wells. Yet when O'Brien travelled to Windfields Farm in Canada in 1968 to buy a yearling for Charles Engelhard, the horse who would be named Nijinsky was not the one he had in mind. He had been advised by Engelhard to look at a Ribot yearling, but the colt did not impress. Another one, however, did. 'While going round the paddocks,' O'Brien told Richard Baerlein, 'I saw a Northern Dancer colt. He was a big, rangy, rather backward-looking horse, and the type who was going to take some time to develop. But I liked him a lot. He had a wonderful set of limbs, a good head and altogether he appealed to me.' The yearling which appealed to O'Brien's all-seeing eye was by Northern Dancer out of Flaming Page, and Engelhard had to go to $84,000 dollars – a Canadian record for a yearling – to secure him.

Never the most straightforward horse to train, Nijinsky on arrival at Ballydoyle posed a problem. He would not eat oats. Vincent O'Brien made contact with Windfields, who told him that the colt was used to being fed horse nuts (which O'Brien had never used), and agreed to send over to Ireland a supply of the required brand. By the time these arrived Nijinsky had consented to eat the Ballydoyle oats.

The details of Nijinsky's career are so familiar as to need little retelling. Unbeaten at two in five races, culminating in the Dewhurst Stakes at Newmarket, he went into the winter of 1969-70 hailed as the best two-year-old in Europe. His first outing in 1970 came in the Gladness Stakes at The Curragh, and he won hard held from the four-year-old Deep Run, who would go on to become an even more potent influence in National Hunt breeding than would Nijinsky on Flat.

He then scored an easy success in the Two Thousand Guineas and headed for Epsom, where his principal rival was the French-trained Gyr, who came with a hefty reputation evidenced by his trainer Etienne Pollet putting off retirement for a year in order to handle the colt. It was the only occasion in Nijinsky's thirteen-race career that he ever started at odds against, but the 11-8 starting price looked generous enough when Lester Piggott eased the horse past Gyr in the closing stages to win convincingly.

Liam Ward, who had ridden Nijinsky in all his races in Ireland, was back in the saddle for the Irish Derby – another easy win. The King George VI and Queen Elizabeth Stakes was the next target, and Nijinsky put up possibly the best display of his life to cruise past the 1969 Derby winner Blakeney and win, without apparent effort, by two lengths. 'I have never been more impressed with a horse,' said his jockey Lester Piggott.

No horse had won the Triple Crown of Two Thousand Guineas, Derby and St Leger since Bahram thirty-five years earlier, and Nijinsky's owner Charles Engelhard was keen to aim his colt at the

The first Triple Crown for an Irish-trained horse is just over three minutes away as Lester Piggott and Nijinsky set off in the 1970 St Leger at Doncaster

Leger. But soon after returning from Ascot to Ballydoyle, Nijinsky contracted ringworm, which caused most of his hair to fall out. The St Leger was on 12 September, and by the end of August he was still unable to engage in proper work. Although he needed a prep race for his final target of the season, the Arc, the St Leger was far from ideal for a horse still suffering the effects of ringworm. But Charles Engelhard was dying and knew it, and was desperately anxious to be remembered as the owner of a Triple Crown winner, so O'Brien was prevailed upon to continue to direct Nijinsky towards Doncaster. The colt duly won the Classic, and with it the Triple Crown, but Lester Piggott felt that the race had got to the bottom of him, and on his return to Ballydoyle Nijinsky was found to have lost twenty-nine pounds in weight. He was clearly not a well horse.

By then there were only three weeks in which to prepare him for the Arc. Gradually his coat recovered and fingers were crossed. But bitter disappointment was lying in wait at Longchamp, for Nijinsky, held well back by Piggott, encountered trouble in running and – like Park Top a year earlier – was switched to the outside. He was eating up the ground in the closing moments of the race as Yves Saint-Martin powered Sassafras towards the winning post and seemed certain to get up, but then he swerved to the left and allowed Sassafras, roused to one final effort by his jockey, to rally and win by a head. (Sassafras was bred in Ireland, and returned there to stand as a stallion.)

In the hope of retiring on a winning note, Nijinsky went to Newmarket for the Champion Stakes, but this highly strung horse was upset by the adulation of the crowd packed around the paddock, became very stirred up and failed to show his true form. Inside the final furlong he moved up to collar the leader Lorenzaccio but could not go through with his effort, and was beaten one and a half lengths.

The desperate anti-climax at the end of Nijinsky's career still smarts. Controversy will for ever linger around Piggott's ride on the colt in the Arc, but his defeat there can surely not be put down to just that one factor. Had he not contracted the ringworm; had he not run in the St Leger; had he not been drawn on the outside in the Arc and thus had difficulty taking up the prominent position his trainer wished to see him in; had he not swerved – a different combination of circumstances would have seen Nijinsky retire unbeaten, and probably acclaimed as the Horse of the Century.

However his stately progress may have ended in a stumble, there was a magic about Nijinsky, and his stud career until his death in 1992 had a similar lustre. He sired a seemingly never-ending succession of top-class horses, including the Derby winners Golden Fleece and Shahrastani. But it is the glory of Nijinsky on the racetrack which is embedded in racing's collective memory – and long may it stay there.

The star of an earlier generation of Irish-trained horses to have left their mark on the European scene, **Ragusa**, also sired a Derby winner – Morston, who took the Blue Riband in 1973.

Ragusa, by the brilliant unbeaten Italian horse Ribot out of Fantan II, was bred by Captain H. F. Guggenheim. A very late foal, he was reared in the fine Irish pastures and balmy climate of the Middleton Park Stud in County Westmeath and should have gone to Captain Guggenheim's trainer in England, Captain Cecil Boyd-Rochfort, but Boyd-Rochfort declined to accept the tiny yearling, and he was sold for just 3,800 guineas to Paddy Prendergast, who bought him on behalf of J. R. Mullion.

He ran once as a two-year-old, winning at The Curragh in October 1962. After running unplaced on his three-year-old debut, he was second in the Dee Stakes at Chester and then stayed on well to come third to Relko in the Derby at 25-1. He was not beaten again that year. After Relko was found to be lame at the start of the Irish Derby and was withdrawn, Ragusa took full advantage of his absence to win comfortably from Vic Mo Chroi. He was then supposed to go for the Gordon Stakes at Goodwood as a preliminary to the St Leger, but when the stable star Noblesse was withdrawn from the King George VI and Queen Elizabeth Stakes, Ragusa took the stage as understudy, and again grabbed the unexpected opportunity for big earnings, winning by four lengths from Miralgo.

In the Great Voltigeur Stakes at York, Ragusa was once more the Prendergast deputy, this time replacing Khalkis, who had been

Ragusa (Garnie Bougoure) saunters home in the 1963 King George VI and Queen Elizabeth Stakes at Ascot, with only Miralgo (Bill Williamson) within striking distance

sidelined by illness, and once more he proved a worthy substitute when beating the Two Thousand Guineas winner Only For Life by a head in a scrambling finish. In the St Leger, for which he was a raging hot favourite at 5-2 on, he was always going well, and pulled clear of his rivals in the straight to win by six lengths – ridden, as he had been in all his big wins, by Garnie Bougoure.

As a four-year-old he had a roller-coaster campaign which did not do as much as had been expected to add to his reputation. Starting at 100-6 on, he beat Credo in the Ardenode Stakes at Naas, but then suffered a major reverse when running third of four in the Royal Whip at The Curragh at odds of 10-1 on. He redeemed himself in the Eclipse Stakes: starting 6-4 on favourite, he came right away from the rest of the field in the straight with Baldric II, the Two Thousand Guineas winner, and stayed on the better to win by one and a half lengths. But he finished his racing career with a poor performance when unplaced behind Prince Royal II and Santa Claus in the Arc.

He was retired to his owner's Ardenode Stud, near Naas, where he died at the early age of thirteen – less than a month before his son Morston won the Derby.

Any horse who could win the Irish Derby, the King George, the St Leger and the Eclipse Stakes must have claims to join the greats, yet there are those nagging doubts about Ragusa. Would he have beaten Relko at The Curragh? Would he have even taken part in the King George had Noblesse been fit? But he could do no more than grasp his opportunity in those races, and that he did with a vengeance. By winning the races he did, he made a major contribution to the growing influence of Ireland on the Flat scene in the 1960s, and he deserves remembering for that.

So, two decades later, does **Stanerra**. In support of a claim to include this grand mare in our brief list of the significant Irish-trained horses since the war, here is Timeform's *Racehorses of 1983*:

To a list of things that improve with age including, according to a Spanish proverb, oil, wine and friends, can now be added the name of Stanerra who has worthy claims to be regarded as one of the best of her sex trained in Ireland over the last twenty-five years. Unbroken at two and seen out only twice at three when trained by Bolger, Stanerra has since improved out of all recognition and as a five-year-old showed form not far behind that displayed by the outstanding Irish-trained Gold Cup winner Gladness at the same age in 1958.

Stanerra, by Guillaume Tell, was owned by Frank Dunne, a successful Irish businessman who took out a trainer's licence in 1982, and by the end of the following year had shown what an Irish-trained horse could achieve in the international arena that racing was rapidly becoming in the 1980s.

Although she played a leading role in that arena in 1983, she had done much to advertise her worth in the previous year. Having won a handicap at The Curragh, she came third in the Hardwicke Stakes at Royal Ascot, ran second to Time Charter in the Sun Chariot Stakes at Newmarket, and was sent to Tokyo to run fourth to Half Iced in the second running of the Japan Cup, beaten just one and a half lengths.

The decision to keep Stanerra in training at five was hugely vindicated. After finishing last in the Earl of Sefton Stakes at Newmarket she was beaten again only twice. In the Brigadier Gerard Stakes at Sandown Park she was ridden for the first time by Brian Rouse, and scored by a length from Ivano. She then went to Royal Ascot, where she pulled off the noteworthy feat of landing the Prince of Wales's Stakes on the first day of the meeting and the Hardwicke Stakes on the fourth – in the latter race cutting down her rivals in the straight and going for home 'with a relish', in the words of *Racehorses*, 'that was a joy to behold'. In the process she broke the course record for twelve furlongs, set by Grundy in the famous King George battle with Bustino in 1975.

Next time out she ran fourth in a muddling race for the Eclipse Stakes, less than a length behind the winner Solford (trained by Vincent O'Brien), but roared back to the winner's enclosure when beating Wassl in the Joe McGrath Memorial Stakes at Leopardstown – the only time she raced in Ireland at five. In the Prix de l'Arc de Triomphe she came sixth behind All Along, beaten about two lengths.

It was then back to Tokyo for the Japan Cup, but international travel has its drawbacks. Peter O'Sullevan recorded Stanerra's training routine during the countdown to the big race:

With four days to the 'off', it looked all of a barrel of saké to a cup of green tea that the 5,000 punts bargain would never make the line-up. Flown out ten days previously on the twenty-hour-plus journey, she had tied up hopelessly and strode out with little more freedom than a hobbled donkey. Her owner-trainer, already renowned for his unorthodox methods, telephoned from Dublin his daily instructions which included six hours' walking per diem. While America's Half Iced (the 1982 winner) and Erin's Isle breezed 1200 metres together; England's Premio Roma winner, High Hawk, and France's Esprit du Nord cantered a course circuit; Italy's Celio Rufo sprinted alongside German hope Tombos, with Canada's Canadian Factor following; and New Zealand's zestful little horse McGinty – so slight in stature he'd need to stand on tip-toe to see over a well-grown bonsai tree – galloped a fast mile, Stanerra, like Felix the cat, just kept on walking.

Stanerra (Brian Rouse) wins the 1983 Hardwicke Stakes from Electric (Walter Swinburn)

The treatment worked gloriously. Starting third favourite behind High Hawk and Esprit du Nord, Stanerra came thundering up the straight to win by a head from the local horse Kyoei Promise.

Stanerra remained in training at six, but after one run when unplaced in the Nassau Stakes at Goodwood was retired.

By no means the best-bred or the most glamorous of the Irish-trained Flat horses whose careers have been described in this chapter, Stanerra none the less demands a place. For by the early 1980s Flat racing at the top level was no longer to be thought of as being confined to the separate parishes of Europe and America. The Japan Cup was designed to bring together the best horses from all corners of the globe, and Stanerra's victory announced that the Irish were not to be left in the departure lounge when the equine jet set started to board.

CHAPTER FIVE

'A Genius with a Horse'

Vincent O'Brien of Ballydoyle

BY THE TIME of the fourth Breeders' Cup race at Belmont Park, New York, on 27 October 1990, the crowd enjoying cold, bright sunshine at the Long Island track had seen enough to last them a while: Dayjur jumping the shadow with the Sprint at his mercy, a scintillating win by Meadow Star in the Juvenile Fillies, and the tragedy of Go For Wand breaking her leg in the final furlong of her unrelenting Distaff battle with Bayakoa. But to cap it all, as the runners for the fourth – the Breeders' Cup Mile – left the paddock, there, sitting grinning on the favourite Royal Academy, was Lester Piggott, whose sensational return to the saddle after retiring in 1985 had taken place just twelve days earlier. Piggott's resumption of race-riding was in itself extra-ordinary, but the real icing on the cake was the way in which his skills seemed to have hardly deserted him. Less than two weeks after five years off, he rode one of the greatest races of his life to get Royal Academy up on the line.

The hullabaloo surrounding Piggott that afternoon tended to obscure the fact that Royal Academy was the first Irish-trained win-ner of a Breeders' Cup race: one of the American television stations even described the horse as trained in England. He was not. He was trained by Vincent O'Brien, and it was highly appro-priate that this landmark in Irish racing history should be credited to the Master of Ballydoyle, who has done more than any other single person to put Ireland in its current place in the racing world.

The connection with the winner of the Mile went beyond simply training him. Royal Academy was a Nijinsky colt selected and bought by Vincent O'Brien as a yearling at Keeneland for $3.5 million and owned by Classic Thoroughbreds, the bloodstock investment company founded by O'Brien, Robert Sangster, John Magnier and Michael Smurfit in 1987 and formally wound up in May 1992. After running a close second to Tirol in the Irish Two Thousand Guineas, he had won the July Cup at Newmarket and run a fast-finishing second to Dayjur in the Ladbroke Sprint Cup at Haydock before heading out to New York.

The Breeders' Cup Mile was Piggott's sixth win in six rides for O'Brien since his comeback – including four in one day at The Curragh earlier that week – and is best described by Vincent O'Brien himself, who had flu and was not able to make the trip:

The Master of Ballydoyle

The field was loaded in order of post position, meaning that we went in first. Perhaps as a result of being in for some time, Royal Academy broke slowly enough and was at least a length last after a furlong. As expected, the pace was very strong for the first half mile and Lester was content to make gradual progress up the outside, leaving him in about seventh position going into the home turn.

Coming out of the bend, Royal Academy just ducked towards the rail for a moment for no apparent reason. This caused him to lose momentum and very nearly cost him the race as it took valuable time for Lester to get him balanced and running again. He still had a good six lengths or so to make up and only a furlong and a half in which to do it; that they managed it at all was a tribute to both horse and rider. To tumultuous cheers from the packed grandstands, Royal Academy got his head in front on the line.

The scenes afterwards were unbelievable; everyone who had ever even set foot in Ireland gave themselves honorary Irishman status for the afternoon and arrived in the winner's enclosure. There were hardened racing veterans with tears in their eyes and the faxes and telephone messages started to come pouring into Ballydoyle. The racing world seemed to realize that something unique had happened that day.

★ ★ ★

Vincent O'Brien's training skills are legendary, and his part in stemming the haemorrhage of the best European bloodstock to the USA was deeply influential in boosting the breeding industry in Ireland and further afield in Europe. It is a measure of O'Brien's importance in the history of Irish racing, and a measure of the crucial part which racing and breeding play in the social and economic make-up of the nation, that in 1983 he received an honorary LLD from the National University of Ireland.

But his magic is beyond simple academic recognition, however well deserved that may be. For followers of racing, there was an aura about an O'Brien runner which was not paralleled by the inmates of any other yard. His remarkable career is rooted in that essential Irish love of the horse, encapsulated by Brough Scott: 'For all his energy and ambition, the real key to Vincent's success lay in something you will never find in books or ledgers, something he was born with, something as Irish as Tipperary: a genius with a horse.'

That genius was bred into him. Born in 1917 in Churchtown, County Cork, he is the son of Daniel O'Brien, a farmer who kept and trained a few horses which he raced for his own enjoyment. Young Vincent spent a year with the trainer Fred Clarke at Leopardstown, then returned to Churchtown and gradually took over training the horses. His first significant success came with a point-to-point mare named White Squirrel, with whom he landed 'a little gamble' in a bumper at Clonmel in 1941; he also rode as an amateur. A far cry from the glory days to come at Ascot and Longchamp, he started breeding and dealing in greyhounds. He took out a trainer's licence in 1943 (having previously contemplated opening a butcher's shop) after his father died, starting his operation with one horse, Oversway, which he had leased from Michael Magnier, John Magnier's grandfather. His first outside owner was the Dublin wool merchant Frank Vickerman, soon to become familiar as the owner of Cottage Rake. In those days you could have a horse in training with Vincent O'Brien for two guineas a week.

The real launching pad for O'Brien's career was a gamble

landed on the Irish Autumn Double in 1944 with Drybob (whom he had bought at Newmarket sales the previous year for 130 guineas) and Good Days. Drybob dead-heated in the Irish Cambridgeshire and Good Days won the Irish Cesarewitch, both starting at 20-1. O'Brien's own investment was modest – £2 each way – but his winnings of £1,000 were enough to give a major boost to his finances when times were hard. Throughout his early years as a trainer he was a fearless backer of his horses when he knew they had a winning chance.

The first horse to thrust Vincent O'Brien into the big time was Cottage Rake, winner of the Cheltenham Gold Cup in 1948, 1949

Vincent O'Brien with work rider Tommy Murphy on the gallops at Ballydoyle

and 1950, shortly to be followed by the triple Champion Hurdler Hatton's Grace. He had made a phenomenal start – three Gold Cups and three Champion Hurdles before he been training a decade. But there were plenty more phenomena before the 1950s were out.

In 1952 began his farming of the Gloucestershire Hurdle at the

National Hunt Meeting at Cheltenham. This race was the equivalent of the novices' hurdle which nowadays opens the Festival programme, and until 1971 was run in two divisions. Division 1 in 1952 was won by O'Brien's runner Cockatoo, ridden by his brother Phonsie (a merciful shortening of Alphonsus Septimus) and starting at 4-1. The complete sequence of O'Brien victories in the Gloucestershire Hurdle is worth marvelling over:

1952 (Div. 1)   Cockatoo (4-1)
1954 (Div. 1)   Stroller (13-8)
1955 (Div. 1)   Vindore (evens)
      (Div. 2)   Illyric (3-1)
1956 (Div. 1)   Boy's Hurrah (9-4)
      (Div. 2)   Pelargos (6-4)
1957 (Div. 2)   Saffron Tartan (11-10 on)
1958 (Div. 1)   Admiral Stuart (6-5)
      (Div. 2)   Prudent King (3-1)
1959 (Div. 1)   York Fair (5-4 on)

His two other runners in the race during this period both finished second.

In 1951 Vincent O'Brien moved from Churchtown to Ballydoyle, near Cashel in County Tipperary – 'At first we made gaps in the fences for the horses to work' – and in 1952 won the Irish Grand National (curiously, for the only time), with Alberoni. The following year he was back winning the Cheltenham Gold Cup with Knock Hard. This was a wonderfully versatile horse, owned by Moya Keogh, owner of Hatton's Grace. Mrs Keogh's husband Harry was an enthusiastic punter, and the stable went for a gamble on Knock Hard in the Irish Cesarewitch in November 1949, only to see the supposed good thing beaten by . . . Hatton's Grace!

In the spring of 1950 Knock Hard took the one-mile Irish Lincolnshire, having been run over fences in his previous race in order to put people off his chance in a highly competitive Flat race. He won the chase, and sauntered home in the Lincolnshire by five lengths at 2-1.

Knock Hard fell at the second last when upsides the eventual winner Mont Tremblant in the 1952 Gold Cup, and in the Manchester November Handicap that year failed by only a head. From there he went to the King George VI Chase, in which he was third behind Halloween and Mont Tremblant.

Even allowing for the fact that the campaigning of the best horses in the early 1950s did not necessarily run along the predictable rails it tends to nowadays, the variety of races in which Knock Hard was asked to run – and often won – is remarkable. But there was a problem. He was diagnosed as having a heart condition, and might drop dead at any minute. Vincent O'Brien warned jockey Tim Molony, 'but he just laughed and said he wasn't worried'. An additional problem was that Knock Hard was not a natural jumper, but despite his dislike of jumping and despite his dodgy heart he won the 1953 Gold Cup well, accelerating up the hill to beat Halloween by five lengths.

In all he won twelve of his forty-three races – four on the Flat, one hurdle and seven chases. As an example of his versatility, consider his spring campaign in 1952: in February, the Baldoyle Chase (fourth); in March, the Cheltenham Gold Cup (fell); in April, the Liverpool Handicap Hurdle (second); in May, a two-mile Flat race at Newmarket (fourth); in June, amateur events on the Flat over twelve furlongs at Lewes and ten furlongs at Worcester, both of which he won.

They don't make 'em like that any more.

The other glowing achievement of Vincent O'Brien's period as a jumping trainer was sending out three consecutive Grand National winners – Early Mist, Royal Tan and Quare Times – between 1953 and 1955.

The lop-eared Early Mist had fallen at the first fence in 1952, but in 1953 was left in the lead before second Becher's and won by twenty lengths from Mont Tremblant.

For Royal Tan, whom Vincent O'Brien rates 'the best jumper of fences I've trained', the 1954 National was third time lucky. Until it was realised that Royal Tan liked to be left alone to make his own decisions about when and how to jump he was a clumsy customer, and had blundered away a winning National chance in 1951, coming second to Nickel Coin. In 1952 he fell at the last when in a

Vincent O'Brien's three Grand National winners: left to right, *Royal Tan (1954), Early Mist (1953) and Quare Times (1955)*

challenging position. He deserved a change of luck in 1954 and got it, getting home by a neck in a driving finish with Tudor Line. Royal Tan was third to ESB in the notorious 'Devon Loch' Grand National in 1956, and in all won eight chases, including the National Hunt Chase at Cheltenham in 1952.

Early Mist and Royal Tan were both ridden to Grand National victory by Bryan Marshall and owned by 'Mincemeat Joe' Griffin – so called because he had made his fortune importing that delicacy into mincemeat-starved England after the war. With the sort of irony with which the history of racing is peppered, Griffin had bought Early Mist at the dispersal sale of the horses of the late J. V. Rank, whose life's ambition had been to win the National.

The going for the 1955 National was so desperate that the water jump had to be omitted. Early Mist and Royal Tan were both in the field – both had been sold on the collapse of Griffin's business empire (perhaps the nation's appetite for mincemeat had its limits) – and Bryan Marshall elected to ride Early Mist, so Pat Taaffe got the ride on Mrs Cecily Welman's Quare Times and won his first National by twelve lengths from the hapless Tudor Line.

In the middle of these great National Hunt exploits, Vincent O'Brien had scored a noteworthy victory on the level when winning the 1953 Irish Derby with Chamier, and his attention began to switch more and more to the Flat. Quare Times's Grand National was his last victory in one of the big chases, though he was still winning the Gloucestershire Hurdle as late as 1959! By the time he gave the training of jumpers up completely in 1959, he had already made his mark in the top flight of European Flat racing with Bally-moss and Gladness. Then in 1960, life suddenly turned very sour.

O'Brien had been in trouble with the authorities before, having been stood down for three months in 1954 over the allegedly in-and-out running of four of his horses, including Royal Tan. In April 1960 the three-year-old colt Chamour was found to have been ad-ministered a stimulant before winning the Ballysax Maiden Plate at The Curragh, and it was announced that O'Brien would have his training licence removed from May 1960 to November 1961. He and his family left Ballydoyle, and brother Phonsie moved in to take over training the horses. Chamour's victory in the Irish Derby that year provoked something akin to a riot at The Curragh as the crowd besieged the Stewards' Room chanting 'We want Vincent!', and after the 'amicable' settlement of a court action in which the trainer had taken the unusual step of suing the Stewards of the Turf Club for libel, the suspension was reduced to a year.

O'Brien's innocence of complicity in administering the stimulant – the analysts pronounced vaguely that the sample contained 'approximately 1/10,000th grain of an Amphetamine derivative re-sembling Methylamphetamine' – was acknowledged by the authorities, but as trainer he had to carry the can.

The case drew attention to the profoundly unsatisfactory manner in which dope samples – saliva and sweat in those days, not urine – were analysed, and one good that came out of the controversy was the arrangement in 1960 between the Turf Club and the Phar-macology Department of Trinity College, Dublin, to have samples more thoroughly analysed.

The Chamour affair also served to illustrate the deep public affection in which Vincent O'Brien was held, and on his return to the racecourse at Leopardstown on 17 May 1961 he was applauded by fellow trainers and mobbed by racegoers.

It did not take him long to pick up where he had left off, and the following year came the first of six triumphs in the Epsom

Derby. Larkspur's victory in 1962 has been overshadowed by the fall of seven horses on the descent to Tattenham Corner, and the fact that he failed to win in three subsequent races leaves him well adrift at the bottom of the list of O'Brien Derby heroes. In the opinion of his trainer, Larkspur's legs probably never fully recovered from racing over Epsom's undulations on firm going.

Larkspur was owned by Raymond Guest, whom O'Brien had met at the Keeneland sales, as was his second Derby winner Sir Ivor in 1968. Then in 1970 came Nijinsky. Two years later saw one of the greatest Derby finishes when Lester Piggott roused Roberto – on whom he had controversially replaced Bill Williamson – to a short-head verdict over Rheingold. (The experts were convinced that Piggott had got to the bottom of the horse, and O'Brien is still amused to recall the jockey's post-race comment to him: 'He wasn't doing a tap in front, you know.') Many British racing fans have never forgiven Roberto for beating Brigadier Gerard at York – the only defeat 'The Brigadier' ever suffered – but on his top form he was a brilliant horse. (Interestingly, Michael Kauntze, who was assistant trainer at Ballydoyle at the beginning of the Seventies, considers Roberto the best of the lot: 'He was a moody bugger and wasn't as consistent as some of the others, but he was very, very good.')

It was in the early 1970s that Vincent O'Brien met John Mulcahy, who advised him that he was selling himself short by training horses for just the training fee and a percentage of the winnings: 'I couldn't believe that this man whom I'd read was the top trainer in the world was getting nothing more than a fee for the expertise he used in picking and training top-class horses.' O'Brien somewhat reluctantly acted on Mulcahy's suggestion that he take at least five per cent of the ownership of any horse he had in training at Ballydoyle.

This led him more into the bloodstock end of the racing business. In 1973 O'Brien had bought two thirds of the Coolmore Stud in Fethard, not far from Ballydoyle, and installed as manager John Magnier (later to marry his daughter Susan), owner of the Castle Hyde Stud in Fermoy, County Cork. Through Magnier, O'Brien became associated with Robert Sangster, and thus was formed the nucleus of the syndicate whose raids on the Keeneland sales

Two eras with Lester Piggott: *left,* after Nijinsky had won the 1970 St Leger, *and* below, *with the rejuvenated jockey at The Curragh in May 1992, on the day that Piggott rode Rodrigo de Triano to victory in the Airlie/Coolmore Irish Two Thousand Guineas, the jockey's sixteenth Irish Classic victory*

'... TRAINED BY VINCENT O'BRIEN, RIDDEN BY LESTER PIGGOTT...'

Vincent O'Brien first met Lester Piggott during the trainer's National Hunt heyday at Cheltenham in the 1950s, but the pair first teamed up with Gladness in the 1958 Ascot Gold Cup. Piggott also rode that great mare to victory in the Goodwood Cup and Ebor Handicap in the same year, and the foundation of one of the great racing partnerships was laid.

Of the sixteen English Classic winners trained by Vincent O'Brien, nine were ridden by Piggott, and the first of these, Valoris in the 1966 Oaks, proved a key moment in the relationship. Noel Murless, who had an informal agreement but no binding contract with the jockey with whom he had won six Classics, had expected him to ride Varinia in the Oaks, but Piggott preferred his chances on O'Brien's filly. He rode Valoris and won, and a month later took the Eclipse for O'Brien on Pieces Of Eight, meanwhile patching up the rift with Murless to the extent that Piggott won the King George for the Warren Place trainer later in July with Aunt Edith.

In 1967 the relationship between O'Brien and Piggott was strengthened through the brilliant two-year-old career of Sir Ivor, and the following year that colt brought glittering victories for the pair in the Two Thousand Guineas, Derby and Washington International. The 1970s saw more Classic success with Nijinsky, Roberto and Boucher before the partnership with Robert Sangster brought along The Minstrel and Alleged and the wonderful achievements of 1977 and 1978.

Trainer and jockey split up in 1980, apparently for a variety of reasons – among them Piggott's dislike of travelling regularly to Ireland and stronger dislike of being committed to riding the Ballydoyle horses even if something better came along – and apparently amicably, and O'Brien was instrumental in encouraging the jockey to make his comeback to the saddle in 1990 after his retirement in 1985 and subsequent imprisonment for tax fraud, meeting Piggott in Dublin and offering him first choice of the Ballydoyle mounts in 1991. At that time John Reid was O'Brien's stable jockey, but a fall from Whippet at the stalls before the Prix de l'Abbaye broke his collarbone, and the sensational return of Piggott was timely.

On 23 October 1990 Vincent O'Brien ran four horses at The Curragh, and asked Lester Piggott – who had returned to the saddle just eight days earlier – to ride. O'Brien recalls what happened:

I was running three two-year-olds and one three-year-old and while I thought they all had a chance, I hardly expected what followed. The first won comfortably; the second fairly easily; the third needed all the assistance Lester could give to get up by a short head and when the fourth horse pulled clear in the final furlong, the reception in the stands and when he returned to the winner's enclosure was tremendous.

Four days later came Royal Academy and the Breeders' Cup Mile. The old partnership was back with a vengeance.

restored to Europe some of the choice bloodlines lost to America in the previous decade. The decision – following the outstanding success of Nijinsky – to go in particular for Northern Dancer blood paid off immediately.

The first group of yearlings bought at Keeneland in July 1975 included Artaius, who would win the Eclipse Stakes and Sussex Stakes, Be My Guest, who would play a crucial role in the establishing of Coolmore as one of the world's great studs – and The Minstrel.

It says much for Vincent O'Brien's instinctive feel for the potential quality of a horse that he was not put off by The Minstrel's colouring, which would have prejudiced many against him. By Northern Dancer, he was a flashy chestnut with a big white blaze – and four large white socks, which would have damned him immediately in the eyes of those judges of horseflesh who held to the old adage:

One white foot, ride him for your life.
Two white feet, give him to your wife.
Three white feet, give him to your man.
Four white feet, sell him – if you can!

Vincent O'Brien was not one to pay any attention to ancient doggerel, and The Minstrel vindicated his judgement. Unbeaten in three races as a two-year-old, including the Dewhurst Stakes, he showed the utmost courage to beat Hot Grove by a neck in the Derby. He then won the Irish Derby and beat Orange Bay by a short head in a desperate finish to the King George VI and Queen Elizabeth Diamond Stakes at Ascot, his last race.

The other great Vincent O'Brien horse of this time, Alleged, by the American sire Hoist The Flag, was beaten only once in ten races, when outgunned in the closing stages of the 1977 St Leger by the Queen's filly Dunfermline. Alleged was the first horse since Ribot to win the Prix de l'Arc de Triomphe twice: in 1977 he benefited from a superb tactical ride from Piggott to beat Balmerino, and a year later beat Trillion (dam of Triptych) by two lengths, again ridden by Piggott.

In 1981 controversy blazed around a colt from Ballydoyle by the

---

VINCENT O'BRIEN'S ENGLISH CLASSIC WINNERS

ONE THOUSAND GUINEAS

1966   Glad Rags

TWO THOUSAND GUINEAS

1968   Sir Ivor
1970   Nijinsky
1983   Lomond
1984   El Gran
        Senor

DERBY

1962   Larkspur
1968   Sir Ivor
1970   Nijinsky
1972   Roberto
1977   The Minstrel
1982   Golden
        Fleece

OAKS

1965   Long Look
1966   Valoris

ST LEGER

1957   Ballymoss
1970   Nijinsky
1972   Boucher

Golden Fleece and Pat Eddery cruise home in the 1982 Derby

name of Kings Lake. Ridden by Pat Eddery (O'Brien's retained jockey), Kings Lake won the Irish Two Thousand Guineas from the English Guineas winner To-Agori-Mou, only for the course stewards to reverse the placings on the grounds of interference. Kings Lake's connections appealed to the Stewards of the Turf Club, and their horse was reinstated as winner (though this was scant consolation to those who had backed the horse and lost their money). The ins and outs of the decision were debated for weeks, and the fuss had not died down when the two colts met in the St James's Palace Stakes at Royal Ascot: this time To-Agori-Mou finished ahead, and the television cameras did not quite catch the gesture which Greville Starkey on the winner made towards Pat Eddery on the runner-up just past the post. They clashed again in the Sussex Stakes at Goodwood, where Kings Lake burst through on the inside to win by a head.

The winner of three Group One races in 1981 – adding the Joe McGrath Memorial Stakes at Leopardstown to the Irish Two Thousand Guineas and the Sussex Stakes – Kings Lake was one of the best milers Vincent O'Brien trained: his other three Sussex Stakes winners were Thatch (1973), Artaius (1977) and Jaazeiro (1978). Thatch also won the July Cup, and other fine sprinters to come from Ballydoyle included Saritamer (Cork and Orrery Stakes and July Cup, 1974), Godswalk (King's Stand Stakes, 1977), Solinus (King's Stand Stakes, July Cup and William Hill Sprint Championship, 1978), Thatching (Cork and Orrery Stakes and July Cup, 1979) and Bluebird (King's Stand Stakes, 1987).

In 1982, five years after The Minstrel, O'Brien won his sixth Derby. Only Robert Robson, John Porter and Fred Darling, each with seven, had trained more winners of the premier Classic, and two of Darling's were in wartime substitute races. No trainer this century has sent out more Derby winners at Epsom than Vincent O'Brien. His sixth winner to make the journey from Ballydoyle to Surrey was Golden Fleece, a Nijinsky colt who ran only four times in his life and was never extended. Golden Fleece did not run again after beating Touching Wood (who went on to win the St Leger) in the Derby: a viral infection and then lameness made it impossible to train him for the big midsummer and autumn races, and he was retired to Coolmore Stud at a valuation of around $25 million. But by the spring of 1984 he was dead with cancer.

Although Golden Fleece ran only once outside Ireland and never had the opportunity to show his true worth against older horses, those closest to him are adamant that he was no unworthy companion to Nijinsky and Sir Ivor in the frame of the greatest O'Brien horses. Pat Eddery, who partnered him at Epsom, considers Golden Fleece as good as any horse he rode. And Vincent O'Brien himself will not be drawn into ranking Sir Ivor, Nijinsky and Golden Fleece into a preferred order.

The following year Caerleon won O'Brien his first French Classic when landing the 1983 Prix du Jockey-Club at Chantilly.

El Gran Senor, next of the famous O'Brien–Sangster horses, would have recorded an untarnished eight-race career but for going down by a couple of inches in the 1984 Derby – a race on which the dust has still not settled.

A son of Northern Dancer, El Gran Senor won four races as a two-year-old, including the Dewhurst Stakes, in which he beat Rainbow Quest. He won the Gladness Stakes at The Curragh on his three-year-old debut, then put up one of the greatest post-war performances in the Two Thousand Guineas when beating Chief Singer by two and a half lengths, a contest whose quality is emphasised by the names of the next two home – Lear Fan and Rainbow Quest. El Gran Senor thus became a hot favourite for the Derby, and were it not for a nagging doubt about his stamina he would have started at odds even shorter than his SP of 11-8 on.

Halfway up the straight El Gran Senor was travelling with an ease that had to be seen to be believed, and in recent memory had been matched only by the contempt with which Shergar had treated his opponents in the Irish Derby. As in that race, the favourite seemed to be part of a film run at a different speed from that in which his rivals were taking part. They were all hammering down the hill, heads thrust out, jockeys scrubbing away or going to work with the whip, while Pat Eddery on El Gran Senor was sitting almost upright, his horse lolloping along, as easy a winner as you could hope to see in the Derby. It was simply a matter of Eddery giving the horse an inch more rein, and El Gran Senor would become the most valuable stallion prospect in the history of the breed.

With the winning post rapidly approaching, only the 14-1 shot Secreto – trained by Vincent O'Brien's 25-year-old son David – was able to keep going strongly, and suddenly it became obvious that El Gran Senor would have to fight for his victory. Inside the final furlong Eddery got down to work and took half a length out of his rival, but Secreto would not be denied, and fought back gamely. The two flashed past the post together, and the photo showed that El Gran Senor had been beaten by a short head.

But it was not over yet. Pat Eddery lodged an objection against Christy Roche on Secreto for 'leaning on my colt inside the final furlong' and a stewards' enquiry was announced. Eventually the 'all right' was given, and Vincent O'Brien had to come to terms with the mixed emotions of deep pride in the achievement of his son in training the Derby winner and deep disappointment that El Gran Senor had gone down.

Eddery came in for criticism over his riding of the favourite – and the story goes that Lester Piggott, passing the disconsolate O'Brien and Sangster after the race, murmured to them: 'Are you missing me?' But the probable explanation is the simplest one – that the colt simply did not quite get home on the day, against a tenacious rival who refused to give in.

Given the question mark over his stamina, there was some surprise when it was decided to aim El Gran Senor at the Irish Derby, but O'Brien explained: 'I felt for the horse's sake that he should have one more chance to prove himself at a mile and a half' – and

Defeat and victory in 1984. Left: Secreto (Christy Roche) just touches off Vincent O'Brien's El Gran Senor (Pat Eddery) in a sensational finish to the Derby. Below: A month later things turn out better as Eddery pushes Sadler's Wells to a brave victory in the Eclipse Stakes from Time Charter (Joe Mercer) and Morcon (Willie Carson)

prove himself he did, winning by a length from Rainbow Quest. He was then retired to stud in the USA, where his offspring have included the 1992 Two Thousand Guineas and Irish Two Thousand Guineas winner, Rodrigo de Triano.

The week after El Gran Senor won at The Curragh, Vincent O'Brien and Robert Sangster won the Eclipse Stakes at Sandown Park with a Northern Dancer colt who was to become the most feted stallion in the world – Sadler's Wells. The following year the stable was badly hit by a virus, and thereafter the flow of winners in big races slowed down as the scale of the training operation at Ballydoyle was reduced. Then in 1990 came Royal Academy and one of the most glorious moments in the whole Vincent O'Brien story. The horse is now a stallion at Coolmore, a near neighbour of Sadler's Wells and Be My Guest.

A few miles away, the 550 acres of Ballydoyle provide eloquent testimony to Vincent O'Brien's mastership of his craft. You rarely get very far when talking or reading about O'Brien before an affirmation that he is the living embodiment of genius as 'an infinite capacity for taking pains', and looking round Ballydoyle, you'd better believe it. There are gallops of different distances, directions, constitutions and undulations. One enables horses to negotiate a left-hand bend similar to Tattenham Corner: here the Derby prospects were tested. There are timing mechanisms built into furlong upon furlong of rails, so that the trainer's intuitive feel for how his horses are working can be glossed by the evidence of the clock. There are viewing stands from which the gallops can be properly observed by the trainer and his partners in the international racing and breeding operation they mastermind. The boxes are spacious and airy, and lined with rubber to minimise the risk of horses getting cast. There are weighing machines and a treadmill, and there is a speaker system through which the horses are treated to music before and after going on to the gallops. And, tellingly, Ballydoyle has its own landing strip, from which horses have been jetted to any number of memorable successes in Europe, and helicopter pad. Ballydoyle is bringing the world to Ireland, and Ireland to the world.

Yet for all the fascination of the training facilities and methods, it is what those methods have achieved under both codes of racing

VINCENT O'BRIEN'S IRISH CLASSIC WINNERS

IRISH TWO THOUSAND GUINEAS

1959   El Toro
1978   Jaazeiro
1981   Kings Lake
1984   Sadler's Wells
1988   Prince Of Birds

IRISH ONE THOUSAND GUINEAS

1966   Valoris
1977   Lady Capulet
1979   Godetia

IRISH DERBY

1953   Chamier
1957   Ballymoss
1970   Nijinsky
1977   The Minstrel
1984   El Gran Senor
1985   Law Society

IRISH OAKS

1964   Ancasta
1965   Aurabella
1969   Gaia
1979   Godetia

IRISH ST LEGER

1959   Barclay
1966   White Gloves
1969   Reindeer
1975   Caucasus
1976   Meneval
1977   Transworld
1980   Gonzales
1985   Leading Counsel
1988   Dark Lomond

for nearly half a century which really boggles the imagination. Contemplate the portraits around the walls of the Ballydoyle dining room, and the photos of so many memorable horses and stirring finishes along the hall, and you feel yourself to be in some sort of equine Nirvana: Cottage Rake, Knock Hard and Hatton's Grace; Early Mist, Royal Tan and Quare Times; Gladness and Ballymoss; Sir Ivor and Nijinsky; Alleged, Golden Fleece and El Gran Senor.

The horses tell the story.

CHAPTER SIX

HORSEMEN FOR COMPANIONS

T HERE IS SOMETHING special about those who live their lives close to the horse, as W. B. Yeats's poem 'At Galway Races' acknowledges:

And we find hearteners among men
That ride upon horses.

Other peoples (the Arabs, for instance) have a special appreciation of the horse: what the French would call a *sens du cheval* and the Irish might describe as the *grá* – the innate love, the feeling in the blood. But nowhere is the horse such a part of the social fabric of the country as in Ireland, and the root of the Irish impact on horse racing is that affinity which breeds so many natural horsemen and women.

A large proportion of Ireland's tiny population grow up with horses, for in what is still primarily an agricultural country it is common for children to be reared on or near farms, and as a consequence to develop an ease and expertise in the handling of horses. It is surely no coincidence that many of the great Irish racing families form mini-dynasties, passing on from father to son the tradition of being a jockey or trainer. Tom Dreaper handed over to his son, as did Dan Moore. Paddy Prendergast's sons took up training. Pat Taaffe came from a great racing family and his son Tom has carried on the tradition. Vincent O'Brien's farmer father trained racehorses, and his son David sent out the 1984 Derby

winner. Then there are the McGraths, the Molonys and the Beas-leys (Harry Beasley was in no hurry to hand over anything: he rode in a race at the age of eighty-five), the Mullinses, the Brogans and the O'Gradys. Pat Eddery, born at Newbridge, County Kildare, in 1952, is the son of the jockey Jimmy Eddery, who won the 1955 Irish Derby on Panaslipper.

In 1982 Pat Eddery achieved the noteworthy feat of winning the Irish jockeys' championship despite being based in England, which of course is where he made his name, and several other jockeys to have made their mark for British trainers since the War are Irish-born. John Reid was born in Ulster (which in terms of racing is not divided from Eire). Richard Dunwoody is also an Ulsterman, one of a stream of fine Irish jump jockeys to have crossed the Irish Sea which includes Bryan Marshall, the stylish Sean Magee (who won the Champion Hurdle on Dorothy Paget's Solford in 1940),

Two famous Irish horsemen greet their winner Danny Connors after the 1991 Coral Golden Hurdle Final at Cheltenham. Trainer Jonjo O'Neill, giving the horse an appreciative pat, was apprenticed at The Curragh and on moving to Britain became one of the most successful jump jockeys of the modern era. He was champion jockey in 1977-8 and 1979-80, on the first occasion notching 149 winners, a total not surpassed until Peter Scudamore topped it in the 1988-9 season. O'Neill never rode the winner of the Grand National, but won the Cheltenham Gold Cup on Alverton (1979) and Dawn Run (1986), and the Champion Hurdle on Sea Pigeon (1980) and Dawn Run (1984). As a trainer he has had success not only over jumps but on the Flat, sending out Gipsy Fiddler to win the Windsor Castle Stakes at Royal Ascot in 1990. Beyond Jonjo O'Neill in the photograph is the owner of Danny Connors, J. P. McManus, proprietor of the Martinstown Stud in County Limerick. A legendary punter, McManus has owned many notable horses, including Jack Of Trumps, Deep Gale and Blitzkrieg

The latest in a long line of top jump jockeys to have come out of Ireland, Adrian Maguire brings Cool Ground back after his last-gasp victory in the 1992 Cheltenham Gold Cup

Tim Molony, Willie Robinson (who won the Grand National, Gold Cup and Champion Hurdle, and was second in the 1958 Derby on Paddy's Point), Ron Barry, Tommy Stack, Jonjo O'Neill, Tommy Carmody, Mark Dwyer and Adrian Maguire.

Countless more well-known jockeys are of Irish descent. Following the troubles of the late 1870s surrounding the issue of Home Rule, Patrick Donoghue joined the swelling exodus across the Irish Sea and arrived in Warrington, Lancashire, in 1882 to work as a puddler in the steel wire works. His son Steve won fourteen English Classics, including the Derby six times, and was champion jockey every year from 1914 to 1923. More recent examples have been Ray Cochrane, of an Ulster background, and Walter Swinburn. Though born in Oxford, Swinburn has a good deal of Ireland in his pedigree. His father Wally was a top Irish jockey, riding what was then a record total of 101 Flat winners in Ireland in 1977. He won the Irish Oaks on Blue Wind in 1981, and retired from the saddle the following year.

There are Irish-born trainers who have made their mark overseas, too, among them – to name just a few – Limerick-born Jim Bentley, who became one of the top trainers in Canada; Atty Persse, born in Galway, trainer of The Tetrarch and of four Classic winners; Cecil Boyd-Rochfort, born in County Westmeath, Royal trainer and winner of thirteen Classics; and, of course, Jimmy Fitz-Gerald. You can take the man out of the bog, as they say, but you cannot take the bog out of the man. Nor, in racing, would you want to.

Add the punters, the priests, the bookmakers and every racegoer who bellows 'Come on, my son!' with an Irish lilt, and you know what Yeats meant when he spoke wistfully of the joy of

> *horsemen for companions,*
> *Before the merchant and the clerk*
> *Breathed on the world with timid breath.*

Beyond dispute the finest trainer of National Hunt horses which Ireland has ever produced is **Tom Dreaper**, through whose hands passed such stars as Arkle, Prince Regent, Flyingbolt, Royal Approach, Fortria, Ben Stack and Fort Leney. If a trainer is to be judged by his horses, Tom Dreaper is incomparable.

He was born in 1898 into a farming family whose interest in racing was minimal, and was well into his twenties before taking up riding in point-to-points: before long he had become one of the finest point-to-point riders in the land. In 1930 his parents pur-chased a 300-acre farm called Greenogue a few miles north of Dublin near Swords, and the following year he took out a public licence, although for the time being his main activity remained farming. He rode Prince Regent when the horse won his first race in 1940.

The story of how Prince Regent came to be trained by Tom Dreaper – literally by accident – has been told in Chapter Three. After that great horse had gone from Greenogue, having brought his trainer a first Irish Grand National in 1942, Dreaper was soon building on his rapidly growing reputation, and in 1949 won the Irish National for the second time with Shagreen.

In those early years he enjoyed the patronage of two major

owners. J. V. Rank owned Prince Regent but never won the Grand National he craved. Third and fourth with his great chaser in 1946 and 1947, he was also the owner of Early Mist, who fell at the first in the 1952 race. By the time of the 1953 running J. V. Rank had died and Early Mist had been bought at the dispersal sale of his horses by Vincent O'Brien on behalf of 'Mincemeat Joe' Griffin. Early Mist put his misfortune of the year before well behind him to win by twenty lengths.

The underbidder for Early Mist at the dispersal sale was Lord Bicester, the other main patron of the Dreaper stable in the early 1950s. By this time those of his horses based in England were trained by George Beeby, and although Dreaper had Roimond in his stable for a while, it was Beeby who had the glory days at Kempton Park when Finnure won the King George in 1949 and at Cheltenham when Silver Fame landed the 1951 Gold Cup.

The best horse that Tom Dreaper trained for Lord Bicester – indeed, one of the best horses he ever handled – was Royal Approach. In the 1953-4 season Royal Approach won six races off the reel, a hurdle followed by five chases, culminating in a facile fifteen-length victory in the Cathcart Challenge Cup at Cheltenham and a brilliant two-length win under 12st in the Irish Grand National at Fairyhouse. Lord Bicester did not take kindly to carping at his horses, and Pat Taaffe, who had become Dreaper's stable jockey in 1950 and rode Royal Approach in all six of his races that season, told the story of how after the Cathcart, the owner was approached by the trainer Jack Anthony. He congratulated Lord Bicester but unfortunately added, 'But he's not much to look at, is he?' – to which the affronted owner replied: 'When did you last look in a mirror?'

The gelding was only six and seemed destined for greatness, but broke a leg while out at grass that summer: although he was able to race again he never recaptured his former brilliance.

It was in 1956 that Tom Dreaper met a lady at Leopardstown races who asked: 'Would you take a horse for me?' Tom's widow Betty (now Lady Thomson) relates how he returned home that evening to tell his wife that the stable had another horse on the way.

'Good. I hope you liked him.'

'I haven't seen him.'

'Do you like the pedigree?'

'Not much, but I liked the look of the girl.'

'The girl' was Anne, Duchess of Westminster, and over the next two decades Tom Dreaper trained ninety-seven winners for her, the first big success coming with Cashel View in the 1959 Galway Hurdle. Apart from Arkle, whose legend has merited a chapter to itself, her most prolific scorer from Greenogue was Ben Stack, who won ten races. Named like Arkle after a Scottish mountain, Ben Stack was a high-class two-mile chaser, winner of the Cotswold Chase at Cheltenham (now the Arkle Chase) in 1963 and of the National Hunt Champion Chase (now the Queen Mother Champion Chase) in 1964, two days before Arkle beat Mill House in the Gold Cup.

Fortria, owned by George Ansley, was a true stalwart of Greenogue in the early 1960s. Though he managed to win the Irish Grand National in 1961 and run second in the Cheltenham Gold Cup both to Mandarin in 1962 and to Mill House in 1963, Fortria was most effective at two miles, winning the Cotswold Chase in 1958, the Champion Chase in 1960 and 1961, and the Mackeson Gold Cup (then also run over two miles) in 1960 and 1962.

Fortria's sire, the 1947 Gold Cup winner Fortina, also produced

He may look like Arkle, but he's Ben Stack: Pat Taaffe in characteristic pose on Tom Dreaper's good two-mile chaser, going away from Irish Imp (Willie Robinson) at the second last in the National Hunt Champion Chase at Cheltenham in 1964

another great Tom Dreaper horse in Fort Leney. Owned by one of Tom Dreaper's best patrons in Colonel (later Sir) John Thomson ('The sort of owner who'll be pleased to come third,' Harry Bonner told Tom), Fort Leney was one of those horses whose achievements in the middle to late 1960s, while the racing world was holding its breath to see whether Arkle would be restored to us, have been rather underrated. The first foal of the renowned broodmare Leney Princess (whose other offspring included Proud Tarquin, Lean Forward, Prince Tino and Tuscan Prince), Fort Leney was a marvellous servant to the stable. Despite a dicky heart, he won fourteen races, including the Leopardstown Chase twice, the Christmas Chase twice, the Thyestes Chase, the Troytown Chase, the Power Gold Cup and the Jameson Gold Cup.

Fort Leney also gave Tom Dreaper his fifth Cheltenham Gold Cup when beating The Laird a neck in 1968 after a stirring battle from the last fence, and followed that with one of his finest races when carrying 12st into second place in the 1968 Whitbread Gold Cup, beaten just a neck by Larbawn. He ended his days at grass on his owner's farm in Oxfordshire, where his grazing companion was none other than Flyingbolt. But old age had mellowed the previously irascible chestnut, and Fort Leney left Flyingbolt in no doubt as to who was boss in their twilight years. This venerable pair stretching over the dry-stone wall to accept titbits from children on their way back from school formed a familiar sight for many years before Flyingbolt had a stroke and was put down in 1983. The following year Fort Leney suffered a heart attack while cantering across the field and died instantly. (By then his owner Sir John Thomson had married Tom Dreaper's widow Betty.)

Perhaps Tom Dreaper's most remarkable feat in the 1960s was to win the Irish Grand National seven years running with seven different horses – Olympia (1960), Fortria (1961), Kerforo (1962), Last Link (1963), Arkle (1964), Splash (1965) and Flyingbolt (1966). In all he won that race ten times.

But he was never able to win the Grand National at Liverpool. Third and fourth with Prince Regent and second with Vulture in 1970 (beaten twenty lengths by Gay Trip), he had plenty of other live candidates for the race – including Owen's Sedge (owned by Gregory Peck), seventh in 1963 – but the nearest he came was with

Black Secret in 1971. Ridden by Tom Dreaper's twenty-year-old son Jim, Black Secret was headed right on the line by Specify and beaten a neck.

Early Mist was not the only Grand National winner to pass through Greenogue before going on to Liverpool glory – though 'glory' might not be quite the word for Foinavon, winner of the 1967 National after the notorious pile-up at the twenty-third fence. Before being sold to Cyril Watkins and going into training with John Kempton in England, Foinavon had been owned by Anne, Duchess of Westminster and trained by Tom Dreaper. Pat Taaffe remembered Foinavon as 'the biggest non-trier I ever rode', though as an exceptionally unflappable horse he was ideal for schooling the young chasers at Greenogue. Early in Foinavon's career, Pat Taaffe assured the Duchess, 'He'll win a National,' but that's the sort of thing jockeys say to owners . . .

One particular incident from Foinavon's days with Tom Dreaper speaks volumes about the horse. As a seven-year-old in January 1965 he started favourite for a handicap chase at Baldoyle, but fell at the third fence, throwing Pat Taaffe clear. In one of those moments which strikes dread into the hearts of racing people, Foinavon failed to rise, but when anxious connections got to the horse they found him gently nibbling at the grass from his recumbent posture. He simply could not be bothered to get up.

Tom Dreaper retired on 31 January 1971. The following day his son Jim took over training the Greenogue horses, with never a hiccough in the progression of big winners. By the end of the 1970s another four Irish Grand Nationals had been added to the Dreaper roll of honour, first with Colebridge in 1974 and then with the redoubtable Brown Lad in 1975, 1976 and 1978. Jim also sent out Ten Up to win the 1975 Cheltenham Gold Cup for the Duchess, and for the first five years of his training career was leading National Hunt trainer in Ireland.

Having nurtured his affinity with horses on the farm and in the hunting field, Tom Dreaper was in many ways the quintessential Irish horseman. Renowned as a judge of livestock, he always thought of himself as a farmer and instinctively put the interests of the horse first. His was not a betting stable, and whatever the circumstances he refused to hurry a horse.

He gave his charges plenty of time to develop and mature, and when they were ready would start them jumping. In *Tom Dreaper and his Horses*, Bryony Fuller has described in fascinating detail his method of teaching his jumpers the rudiments of their craft:

The country around Greenogue is ditch country and the young-sters were introduced to jumping over open ditches. Tom had the young horse bridled and put on a cavesson with a long rope. He was led up to the edge of an open ditch where he was held and allowed to have a good look into and across the ditch. The man holding the horse threw the rope across the ditch to a couple of lads waiting in the landing field. The horse was encouraged to bring his hind legs up to his front legs and then made to jump the open ditch from a stand, using his hocks to produce propulsion. After he had repeated this a few times, the horse did it quite calmly and walked up to the edge, settled himself and took off.

The next stage in the horse's education was over baby bush fences where he was lunged around and around, jumping the fences slowly in each direction. Only when the horse was jumping open ditches and bush fences sensibly, using his hocks properly, was he ridden over fences.

For Dreaper, jumping was the key to the whole operation, and un-like many trainers he believed in schooling his charges twice a week to keep their jumping muscles in trim. He also insisted on keeping his horses fresh, and never had them out on the gallops for longer than was necessary.

As with Fulke Walwyn, greatest of the English jumping trainers, the Dreaper horse tended to be of a certain stamp – tall and well built, with plenty of bone, good heart room and a bold eye. The objective was to turn them into chasers. For Dreaper, hurdling was simply an important step in the education of a young horse for steeplechasing – a means to an end. It is significant that of the twenty-six races which he won at the National Hunt Meeting at Cheltenham, only one was in a hurdle – and that, Division 1 of the 1964 Gloucestershire Hurdle, was part of Flyingbolt's education for chasing.

Though unassuming and completely dedicated to his horses,

Dreaper had a dry wit and a fierce loyalty, and the two came together when he was asked by a steward at Hurst Park whether he was satisfied with the riding of Pat Taaffe. His reply: 'I have worse at home.'

Tom Dreaper died in 1975.

The death of **Pat Taaffe** on 7 July 1992 robbed not only Ireland but all steeplechasing of one of its most loved and admired characters. The jockey whose achievements on such horses as Arkle, Flyingbolt and Fort Leney have been chronicled elsewhere in this book tasted success all but unparalleled in his profession but remained modest, unassuming, and endearingly ready to talk about all the great horses with which he was associated.

Son of the trainer Tom Taaffe (who won the 1958 Grand National with Mr What), Pat was born in Rathcoole, County Dublin, in 1930, and learned his riding skills through hunting and show jumping. He rode his first point-to-point winner – Merry Coon at the Bray fixture – in 1946 while still a schoolboy, and then progressed to riding under Rules as an amateur. His first winner was on a chance ride picked up at Phoenix Park on Easter Saturday 1946:

I was engaged to ride a horse called Curragh Chase and I told some of the lads that I expected to win. On the morning of the race Curragh Chase was sold and I was given a spare ride on another horse, Ballincorona, which won the race at 20-1, beating Curragh Chase. Fortunately I hadn't told my pals the name of the horse I originally expected to ride and they were unaware that any change had taken place.

At the two-day Christmas meeting at Leopardstown in 1949 he won four races – including one on Tom Dreaper's Shagreen – and was informed by the stewards that if he wished to continue riding under Rules he should turn professional. His father, discussing this prospect with Tom Dreaper, expressed concern that Pat would be hanging around the weighing room looking for rides, so Dreaper said that need not happen – he could ride for him.

Thus began one of the most successful and enduring partnerships which National Hunt racing has ever seen, one in which
Taaffe won every major steeplechase at least once. His association
with Arkle is of course the stuff of racing legend, and during his
time with Dreaper he won countless other big races on the Greenogue stars. Yet ironically, although Tom Dreaper was never to land
the Grand National, Pat Taaffe won it twice. In 1955 he rode Quare
Times, the last of Vincent O'Brien's three winners; his brother Tos
was third on Carey's Cottage, trained by their father. Pat won his
second National as a forty-year-old in 1970 on Gay Trip, trained by
Fred Rimell, whose stable jockey Terry Biddlecombe had been
badly injured the previous month and had to forgo the ride.

The Irish Grand National fell six times to Pat Taaffe, with Royal
Approach (1954), Umm (the 1955 winner, a half brother to Foinavon), Zonda (1959), Fortria (1961), Arkle (1964) and Flyingbolt
(1966), and he was champion jockey in Ireland in 1952 and 1953.

But he also suffered the other side of a jump jockey's life. Riding
a horse named Ireland in a hurdle at Kilbeggan in August 1956, he
took a terrible fall and fractured his skull. A rumour swept round
Dublin that Pat Taaffe had been killed, and even when the extent
of his injuries became known, it was widely assumed that he
would not ride again. But he was back race-riding at Navan on 14
November, only to fall again, needing stitches in a leg. Three days
later he was due to ride two Dreaper horses in important races at
Manchester and, worried about his fitness, asked the trainer
whether it would not be more sensible to find another jockey for
them.

'If you don't ride them we won't run them,' replied Dreaper.
Taaffe rode both, and both won.

On his retirement in 1970 Pat took up training from his yard at
Alasty, near Naas, where far and away the best horse he handled
was the erratically brilliant Captain Christy.

If the abiding memory of Arkle is of his ears, that of his regular
partner is of his elbows, jutting out as they urged yet another
Dreaper winner towards the last fence. Although he may not have
been the most stylish rider of a finish ever seen on a racecourse,
he was possibly the greatest horseman of all in a golden age of
jump jockeys. A steeplechase is as often won out in the country as

in a rousing drive to the line, and Taaffe's ability to get horses making the best use of themselves throughout a race and making lengths with their jumping was as effective as any stylish Flat-race finish.

With his tall, lanky physique – its apparent inelegance accentuated by his riding very short for a steeplechase jockey – Pat Taaffe cut an unmistakable figure. But it was his complete horsemanship which endeared him to the racing community, who turned out in force three days after his death to pack St Brigid's Church in Kill, County Kildare, for the memorial mass. A measure of the regard with which this most humble of men was held in his native country was the presence of a representative of the Taoiseach (prime minister). Willie Robinson, Taaffe's great friend and rival from the glory days of Arkle and Mill House, gave one of the readings. Martin Molony was there, and other great jockeys including Aubrey Brabazon, T. P. Burns and Tommy Carberry.

In his homily, Father Paddy Fitzsimons quoted Ted Walsh's tribute to Pat Taaffe: 'As gentle as a lamb off a horse, a lion in the saddle.'

★ ★ ★

Ask Pat Taaffe which of his fellow jump jockeys he most admired, and the name **Martin Molony** was soon aired. Ask Vincent O'Brien which jump jockey he holds in the highest esteem, and the reply is: 'Martin Molony was as good as any I've seen.'

Although, unlike his elder brother Tim, he was never champion jockey in England, Martin Molony held the racing public on both sides of the Irish Sea in thrall. Like Taaffe and so many other Irish jockeys, he started to ride very young (at the age of seven in his case) and gained invaluable experience accompanying his parents out hunting. When he was thirteen he was apprenticed to Martin Hartigan, through whose hands, years earlier, the young Gordon Richards had passed. Under Hartigan he learned the jockeyship to complement his horsemanship, a combination which paved the way to a career under both codes.

His first winner was on the Flat – Chitor at The Curragh in October 1939 – but as his weight rose he gradually mixed Flat rides with National Hunt. He was champion jump jockey in Ireland

Martin Molony brings Silver Fame back after winning the 1951 Gold Cup

for the first time in 1946 (sharing the title with Aubrey Brabazon), and thereafter every year until his career was prematurely cut short after fracturing his skull in a fall from a horse named Bursary at Thurles in September 1951, when he was twenty-six. Pat Taaffe took over as leading jockey in 1952.

In his short career Martin Molony displayed a versatility remarkable even by the standards of Irish racing. In 1950 he came third in the Oaks at Epsom on Stella Polaris. He won several Irish Classics, including the 1951 Irish Two Thousand Guineas on Signal Box, on whom he was also third to Arctic Prince in the Derby. In 1949 and 1950 he won the Irish Cesarewitch on Hatton's Grace, though he did not ride that horse to any of his Champion Hurdle victories. He landed the Irish Grand National three times, on Knight's Crest (beating Prince Regent in 1944), Golden View II (1946) and Dominick's Bar (1950).

His biggest individual victory, and for many who saw him in action the finest ride of his career, came on Lord Bicester's strapping chestnut Silver Fame, whom he rode to a short-head victory over J. V. Rank's Greenogue in the 1951 Cheltenham Gold Cup. The two jumped the last fence alongside Lockerbie, who weakened on the run-in leaving Greenogue and Silver Fame to fight out a finish so close that there are still people around who think that the judge chose the wrong horse. (There was no photo finish at Cheltenham in those days.)

Martin Molony was a fearless rider, with a famous sense of balance and a particular skill at putting his mount at the final fence. 'Go with your horse,' his father had taught him in the hunting field, and the advice paid off time and time again on the racecourse.

A teetotaller, he is deeply religious and chose to live a quiet life. He could have made a great deal more money by riding in England but he always declined to do so, preferring to commute by aeroplane when his commitments demanded it. During the 1950-1 season, when he was winning on one in every three rides in England, the coach for Dublin airport would go from outside Dave O'Leary's pharmacy in Cathal Brugha Street. On seeing Martin Molony get off the coach after yet another successful raid, the proprietor would remark: 'There's Molony again. The banks can't open soon enough for him to bank his money.'

Martin's brother **Tim Molony** was better known in England, where he was leading National Hunt jockey four years in succession from 1948-9 to 1951-2, and again in 1954-5. He won the Gold Cup on Knock Hard in 1953, and the Champion Hurdle four years in succession, on Hatton's Grace (1951) and three times on Sir Ken (1952-4), though he never won the Grand National. In all he won some 900 races. John Lawrence (Lord Oaksey) captured the essence of his skills:

Tim Molony learnt to ride in the Irish hunting field – and acquired there a relaxed, almost casual looking seat which made him, of all the great jockeys I have been privileged to watch, perhaps the hardest to dislodge. Strong as an ox, he was blessed too with a pair of hands which could make the hardest puller look like

Tim Molony goes to post

a child's pony. He rode long by modern standards and was in his element on bad or inexperienced jumpers – attacking each fence as if it was an enemy, kicking harder and harder the more mistakes they made and winning dozens of races by a length or less gained somewhere far out in the country where the horseman comes into his own.

On the Flat the early 1950s were noteworthy for the steep rise in the fame and fortunes of **Paddy Prendergast**. He too came from a background full of horses, and his father 'Old Paddy' was a notable 'spotter' of mounts: tell him what you wanted and how much you could afford, and he would find you the right horse. The late Roger Mortimer recalled: 'For £60 he produced for me a plain, powerful long-backed mare who looked like an empty bus.'

Paddy Prendergast – widely known as 'P.J.' or 'Darkie' – was born in 1909. He rode for a while over the jumps in England, withoutconspicuous success, and turned to training in 1940 with just two horses. In 1950 he won his first Irish Classics: the Irish One Thousand Guineas with Princess Trudy, followed by the Irish Derby with Dark Warrior. Unsurprisingly, he was champion trainer in Ireland that year, a feat he achieved seven times in all. In 1963 he became the first Irish trainer ever to top the trainers' list in Britain, and he held the title in 1964 and 1965 to better the

record even of Vincent O'Brien, who headed the list just twice.

He had his first winner in England in 1945, but it was in 1950, that great year in Ireland, when he really made his presence felt across the water too, with Windy City winning the Gimcrack Stakes at York and heading the Free Handicap in England and Ireland. Prendergast had a wonderful record in the top English two-year-old races, winning the Gimcrack four times, the Champagne Stakes at Doncaster five times, and the Coventry Stakes at Royal Ascot six times.

His first winner in an English Classic was Martial in the 1960 Two Thousand Guineas, and by 1964 he had trained a winner of every English Classic except the Derby. He never did train a Derby winner, though Meadow Court was second to Sea Bird II in 1965 and Ragusa third to Relko in 1963; yet he dominated the mid-Sixties in England, and it is worth looking at how he did so.

Paddy Prendergast's wonderful filly Noblesse (Garnie Bougoure) winning the 1963 Oaks by ten lengths

In 1963 he had three star turns. Ragusa won the King George VI and Queen Elizabeth Stakes and the St Leger, Khalkis won the Eclipse and Noblesse landed the Oaks. Noblesse was an outstanding filly. She won twice at two, the more notable success coming in the Timeform Gold Cup at Doncaster, and at three landed the Musidora Stakes at York with very little effort before becoming one of the easiest winners ever of the Oaks. Ridden by Garnie Bougoure, she sailed home by ten lengths, a winning distance for that Classic only once exceeded. She was then beaten in the Prix Vermeille and retired.

In 1963 Prendergast also won four Classics in Ireland, where he added the trainers' championship to the English.

Paddy Prendergast's 1964 campaign in England saw Pourparler winning the One Thousand Guineas, Ragusa the Eclipse, Linacre the Queen Elizabeth II Stakes at Ascot and Hardicanute the Timeform Gold Cup, but the 1965 title he took without winning any of the English Classics – thanks mainly to Meadow Court winning the King George VI and Queen Elizabeth Stakes and Carlemont the Sussex Stakes.

Paddy Prendergast, second only to Vincent O'Brien in pushing Ireland to the forefront of racing in Europe, died in 1980.

★ ★ ★

Paddy Mullins may be best known as the trainer of Dawn Run, but in a long career he has handled many other well-known horses, including Hurry Harriet, who beat Allez France in the 1973 Champion Stakes; four winners of the Irish Grand National (Vulpine (1967), Herring Gull (1968), Dimwit (1972) and Luska (1981)); and Grabel, who won the Dueling Grounds International Hurdle in Kentucky in 1990

Two current trainers in particular are maintaining the momentum established by O'Brien and Prendergast. Son of the trainer Charlie Weld, the Surrey-born **Dermot Weld** qualified as a vet and rode as an amateur – he was champion amateur in Ireland three times – before taking out his first training licence in 1972 after spells as assistant to his father and to Tommy Smith in Australia.

By the end of 1991, Weld had been champion trainer in Ireland fifteen times on the basis of number of winners trained, and five times on the basis of prize money won. That year he set a new Irish record: the 150 winners (120 Flat, 30 National Hunt) he sent out from Rosewell House, by The Curragh, beat the 148 registered in 1990 by Jim Bolger – whose achievement smashed the record 135 wins notched up by the famous Senator J. J. Parkinson in 1923.

Dermot Weld with Executive Perk

Though Weld became in 1989 the first Irish trainer to top the £1 million mark in prize money, it is his international wins which have accelerated the rise of Ireland as a force to be reckoned with in Flat racing. He took his first English Classic with Blue Wind, seven-length winner of the 1981 Oaks, and made his mark in France when sending out Committed to win the Prix de l'Abbaye in 1984 and 1985; he has twice won the important Premio Parioli in Rome; and in 1991 his Additional Risk took the Hong Kong Invitation Bowl. But Dermot Weld's most significant contribution to the Irish cause came when Go And Go, a son of the Coolmore stallion Be My Guest, won the Belmont Stakes in New York in June 1990 under Michael Kinane to become the first European-trained horse ever to land any of the American Triple Crown races.

It was fitting that Weld should have been the trainer responsible for this historic occasion, as he had been notably adventurous in going for the big American prizes – Go And Go had won the Laurel Futurity and run in the Breeders' Cup Juvenile as a two-year-old – and had long nurtured the ambition to win the Kentucky Derby or the Belmont. To win the latter had an added spice for the trainer, as he had worked at Belmont Park in the backstretch as a vet twenty years before.

Starting at 15-2, Go And Go won the Belmont Stakes by the wide margin of eight and a quarter lengths from Thirty Six Red, with the Kentucky Derby winner Unbridled fourth. His Irish jockey, Michael Kinane, thus forged another link in a remarkable chain of international victories: in the twelve months before the Belmont he had won the Irish Oaks on Alydaress, the Cartier Million at Phoenix Park on The Caretaker and the following day the Prix de l'Arc de Triomphe on Carroll House, and then in May 1990 the Two Thousand Guineas on Tirol. And seven weeks after the Belmont he was to take the King George VI and Queen Elizabeth Diamond Stakes on Belmez. Kinane was in the saddle when Dermot Weld's Brief Truce became the first Irish-trained Group One winner in England in 1992 when landing the St James's Palace Stakes at Royal Ascot.

But Weld's achievements are not to be judged only by victories in the classiest races. He was the first Irish trainer to win the Lincoln Handicap (Saving Mercy in 1984), and he has had many notable jumping successes – with the likes of Perris Valley, winner of the 1988 Irish Grand National, Rare Holiday, who won the Triumph Hurdle at Cheltenham in 1990, and that grand chaser Greasepaint, second in the Grand National in 1983 and 1984.

Like Dermot Weld, **Jim Bolger** had his first Classic success in England in the Oaks, but whereas Weld's Blue Wind started favourite, Bolger's 1991 winner Jet Ski Lady was the rank outsider

Jim Bolger greets Christy Roche and St Jovite after their stunning victory in the 1992 Budweiser Irish Derby at The Curragh

at 50-1. Her performance belied those odds comprehensively as, ridden by Christy Roche, she led all the way and in the straight simply came away from her rivals to win by ten lengths.

Now based at Coolcullen, Carlow, Jim Bolger is from a farming but not a racing background in Wexford, and he spent some time working as an accountant in Dublin before taking out his first training licence in July 1976. Since then he has done especially well with fillies: apart from Jet Ski Lady, he has trained such good horses as Flame Of Tara (winner of the Coronation Stakes and dam of Salsabil and Marju), Condessa (who won the Yorkshire Oaks), Give Thanks and Park Express. But the horse who really propelled Bolger into the big league was a colt – St Jovite. The trainer had expressed great hopes for this son of Pleasant Colony – 'I will not be surprised to hear him described as awesome from another continent when he moves to middle distances,' he told the *Irish Racing Annual* – and his faith was rewarded with a staggering performance in the Budweiser Irish Derby, when St Jovite came right away from the Derby winner Dr Devious (who had beaten him into second place at Epsom) to win by twelve lengths. In his next race St Jovite was even more awesome, demolishing a high-class field in the King George at Ascot.

In 1990 Bolger was champion trainer by winners and Weld champion by prize money. In 1991 these positions were reversed. The keen rivalry between the two has its lighter side, as Tony O'Hehir reported in the *Racing Post*:

There is even a well-aired Bolger–Weld joke. The one about Weld arriving at the pearly gates and seeking, and receiving, assurance from St Peter that Bolger has not arrived before him.

But on a stroll through heaven Weld discovers a magnificent palace, named Coolcullen and painted in purple and white (Bolger's racing colours).

WELD: 'I thought you said Jim wasn't here.'

ST PETER: 'He isn't here.'

WELD: 'But I saw a mansion named Coolcullen. He must be here.'

ST PETER: 'You're wrong. God lives there. He only thinks he's Jim Bolger.'

CHAPTER SEVEN

'WHY DO PEOPLE FISH IN STREAMS?'

THE BREEDING BUSINESS IN IRELAND

WHEN SIR WILLIAM TEMPLE was making his representation to the Lord Lieutenant in 1673 on how breeding good bloodstock could benefit the Irish economy, he wrote:

In the studs of persons of quality in Ireland where care is taken and cost is not spared, we see horses bred of excellent shape and vigour and size.

'Care is taken and cost is not spared': what would Sir William have made of Coolmore or Kildangan?

Coolmore Stud, near the town of Fethard in deepest Tipperary, reeks of quality. From the very entrance, between imposing stone pillars and ornate ironwork, past the large bronze of the stallion Be My Guest to the offices clicking with the elaborate technology on which today's multi-million-dollar bloodstock operations depend as much as on the lush emerald pastures which stretch for mile upon mile outside, Coolmore is a place steeped in the notion that if a thing is worth doing, it is worth doing well.

You don't have to linger long in the reception area at Coolmore to be reminded what the whole operation is about: breeding champion racehorses. Playing on the television screen in the corner is a promotional video running some of the greatest racing performances of the resident stallions and their offspring. Settle back and enjoy a compilation of some of the most memorable racing moments of recent years – Generous slamming his field in the Derby, Scenic and Prince Of Dance fighting out that gripping Dewhurst dead heat, Tirol battling home in the Two Thousand Guineas and then the Irish Two Thousand – and the runner-up at The Curragh that day, Royal Academy, winning the July Cup, running second to Dayjur at Haydock (and shouldn't he have got closer?) and then staging that unbelievable late run under Lester Piggott to land the Breeders' Cup Mile. Like the Grand National finish between Crisp and Red Rum, every time you watch a video of the Belmont Park race you cannot quite believe that it will end in the result it did, and – happily, for the opposite reason – it remains compelling viewing.

Visit the Coolmore stallion boxes, and the impression of quality and class deepens. Around three sides of a perfectly kept lawn with adjacent flower beds are neatly ranged what look like small white pebble-dashed holiday cottages. It is when you read the names above the doors that the importance of Coolmore in the modern bloodstock industry really comes home. Move respectfully down past the likes of Last Tycoon, Tirol and Royal Academy, whom you have just been cheering home on the video, and you come to three boxes forming a kind of millionaires' row. The one

The stallion boxes at the Coolmore Stud

on the left is home to Sadler's Wells, champion sire in 1990 and, as the acknowledged heir of his sire Northern Dancer, the most valuable horse in the world: 'worth £40 million', they say, but such a sum is too difficult to comprehend. In the middle is Be My Guest, champion sire in 1982 and subject of that statue near the entrance. And on the right is Caerleon, champion sire in 1988 and 1991, which is a cold statistic, and sire of Generous, which is not.

There are other familiar faces around: the good sprinters Danehill and Bluebird, the Irish Derby winner Law Society, the Royal Lodge winner High Estate, Scenic, a son of Sadler's Wells viewed on that video dead-heating with another Sadler's Wells colt in the Dewhurst, the St James's Palace Stakes winner Persian Heights. And there is Classic Music, a charming fellow who never raced but has the great good sense to be a full brother to Sadler's Wells. Never having seen a racecourse despite having been the most expensive yearling ever sold in Britain when fetching 2,800,000 guineas in 1988, he is something of an unknown quantity, but he has the same breeding as the most important sire of the lot and his services can be bought for 2,750 guineas, as opposed to 100,000 guineas for Sadler's Wells.

It is this concentration of quality which really sets the visitor to Coolmore drooling, and the feeling continues on a drive around the rolling green acres to see the mares in their barns or turned out in their paddocks. Time Charter has just left, though her famous name still adorns her empty box in one of the many separate barns where the mares stay, and Oh So Sharp comes as necessary on a day trip from the Kildangan Stud up in Kildare. But there, calmly picking grass at the edge of one paddock, is Flame Of Tara, dam of Salsabil and Marju. In another paddock a middle-aged brown mare ambles around with her foal by Sadler's Wells but resolutely refuses to come and greet her admirers: she must have plenty, for this is Detroit, winner of the Arc in 1980. She looks sniffily at her visitors and canters away, her foal gangling along half a length adrift. You wonder whether the next time you see that little fellow will be in the parade ring at Ascot.

Mares and foals are not the only livestock in the paddocks. Some 2,500 head of cattle are kept at Coolmore, not to add a few extra quid to the turnover but to play their part in the ecosystem which is as essential a part of the stud as any mobile phone. The cattle are there to improve the fertility of the soil: used bedding from the horses serves as bedding for the cattle during the winter, and the manure which results, once decomposed, is applied as fertiliser to the pastures the next autumn. Thus the use of chemical fertilisers is avoided, and the cattle manure produces a rich pasture, to the obvious benefit of the grazing horses. There are also sheep, marshalled to clean the paddocks during late autumn and early winter.

A symbol, and in many ways the flagship, of the resurgence of Ireland as a place where the world's finest bloodstock can be bred, Coolmore itself is but one member of a family of sixteen studs in Ireland and others in Australia and the USA – where in Kentucky stand El Gran Senor, Lomond, Storm Bird, Seattle Dancer and Woodman. Because the covering season in the southern hemisphere is much later in the year than that in the northern, several of the Coolmore stallions will be shipped to Australia during the Irish summer so that their services may be available to Australian breeders, returning in good time for the resumption of duties in Tipperary on 15 February. In such a manner does Irish bloodstock exert a global influence.

The Coolmore group of studs was founded in the mid-1970s when Robert Sangster teamed up with Vincent O'Brien and John Magnier, widely acknowledged as one of the cleverest brains in the bloodstock industry, with a plan to change the face of breeding. They would buy well-bred yearlings not simply to race – though the expertise of O'Brien would ensure that their capabilities on the course were exploited to the full – but as potential stallions: if the colt had both a pedigree and a racing record of a high order it would become a highly valued asset and, on the basis of top-class racecourse performance, extremely desirable for syndication among the high rollers of the racing and breeding game. Vincent O'Brien, than whom there was no finer judge of a yearling in the world, directed them towards the Northern Dancer family following his experience with Nijinsky, and from the first crop of yearlings bought at Keeneland in 1975 came the dual Derby winner and King George winner of 1977, The Minstrel. He had cost $200,000 as a yearling in Kentucky; when he returned there to stand as a stallion he was syndicated at a valuation of $9 million. Some start!

The arrival of the Maktoums in international racing altered the picture and made the best-bred yearlings exceedingly expensive to buy at the sales. Sangster lost out to Sheikh Mohammed in the almost incredible sale of a Northern Dancer yearling for $10.2 million at Keeneland in 1983, and would have had his own thoughts about the subsequent career of that horse, named Snaafi Dancer: it failed to make even one appearance on the track, then proved useless at stud. But though the sum involved may have been scarcely more than small change to Sheikh Mohammed, the stakes had been raised hugely, and Sangster could no longer hope to compete in the sale ring.

Coolmore's wealth of Northern Dancer blood, however, was to prove a great and enduring asset, especially after the great stallion himself died in November 1990. The special quality of his stock is twofold, says Coolmore's general manager Bob Lanigan: 'On the racing side, they are tough and sound, and these attributes dovetail with Northern Dancer's ability to consistently produce correct, good-looking horses.' He was a phenomenal sire, and a great sire of sires – notably Nijinsky, El Gran Senor, and Sadler's Wells. Coolmore has several sought-after sons of Northern Dancer and is thus in a very strong position in the international bloodstock business, and above all it has probably the most important sire in the world.

'Sadler's Wells is going to be the sire of the '90s and probably a better sire than Northern Dancer himself.' Such was the opinion of breeding expert Tony Morris, and certainly the early crops of this supremely tough racehorse bore out such a view. Scenic and Prince Of Dance, Dewhurst dead-heaters, were both his sons, Old Vic won the Prix du Jockey-Club and the Irish Derby, and In The Wings the Coronation Cup and the Breeders' Cup Turf. His second crop included the marvellous Salsabil, winner of the One Thousand Guineas and the Oaks in 1990 and the first filly to win the Irish Derby since 1900. Twenty years ago a horse of Sadler's Wells' achievements on the track – trained by Vincent O'Brien to win the Irish Two Thousand Guineas, the Eclipse Stakes and the Phoenix Champion Stakes – would have been sold to stud in America, and the fact that the Coolmore set-up made it possible for him to

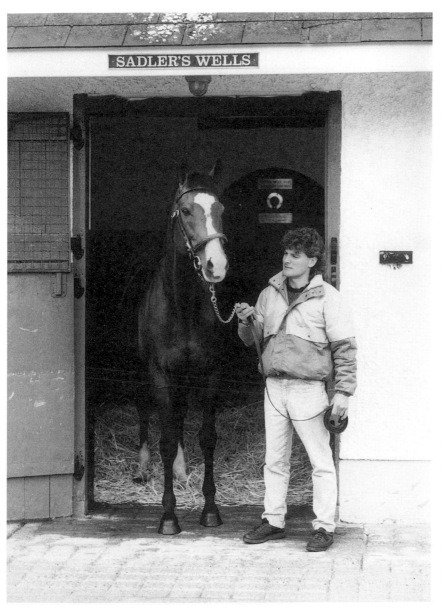

The name above the door says it all ...

remain in Ireland is a great boost for the profile of Irish breeding. Sadler's Wells looks like becoming the king of stallions, and with Generous's sire Caerleon just two boxes away, the breeders of the world will keep beating a path to Tipperary, and Tipperary stock will spread the virtues of Irish breeding far and wide; in spring 1992, for example, fifteen Coolmore yearlings were exported to Russia.

The Goffs sale ring at Kill, County Kildare. Goffs, the leading Thoroughbred sales company in Ireland, was founded by Robert Goff, appointed official auctioneer to the Turf Club in 1866. In 1887 the first Goffs sale took place in Ballsbridge, Dublin, from where were later sold the likes of Easter Hero, Golden Miller, Prince Regent, Arkle and Red Rum. In 1975 Goffs moved to a huge new complex at Kill (near Naas), where it caters chiefly for the yearling market. Goffs' only rival in Ireland is the Irish branch of the leading British bloodstock auctioneers Tattersalls, now based in ultra-modern premises by Fairyhouse racecourse in County Meath and selling mainly to the National Hunt market

★   ★   ★

The factors which make Ireland such a good place for breeding Thoroughbreds are of course manifold. We have seen earlier the natural benefits to the growth of bone – and therefore soundness – bestowed by the limestone-rich land and water, and the temperate but moist climate is ideal for rearing youngstock. As with the land, so with the people: a population versed in the ways of the horse adds to the attractions of Ireland for breeders.

Not least of the incentives to breed and rear young horses here are the tax breaks bestowed by a government well aware that breeding is not some exotic frippery for the rich but a highly important part of the country's economy, bringing in a large amount of foreign investment. Since the late 1960s, on an initiative of the then Minister of Agriculture Charles Haughey (himself a breeder and enthusiastic man of the Turf), income tax is not payable in Ireland on profits made by stallion owners (nor, by the same token, are losses tax-deductible). Haughey's remarks in his address to the survey team appointed for the horse breeding industry in 1965 are worth quoting for the way they illustrate the importance of the bloodstock business to Ireland:

Traditionally, the horse has been a part of the Irish way of life. In many parts of the world, the name of Ireland is known only through the reputation of her horses and the prestige of Ireland is closely linked with the quality of the horses we send out to all parts of the world.

Twenty-five years later, as Taoiseach, Haughey sent a message to the 1990 edition of *The Irish Thoroughbred* which focused on Thoroughbred breeding:

Natural advantages in climate and soil and favourable taxation treatment have contributed to the development of our excellent reputation for horse breeding. However, it is the skill and innate love of horses in our breeders that have been the decisive factors.

The Thoroughbred breeding industry has long been an established feature of many Irish farms. One or two mares have traditionally been kept to produce foals intended for Flat or National Hunt racing. In more recent times we have seen the development of large specialised stud farms. I consider this to be a positive development and complementary to the work of the small breeder.

Such pronouncements are indicative of the stress which successive Irish administrations have placed on the breeding industry as a significant component of the country's agricultural industry, meriting government support. In addition to the tax incentives for a stallion owner to stand his horse in Ireland rather than overseas, VAT on bloodstock is extremely low: in August 1992 the rate levied was 2.7 per cent, compared with 5.5 per cent in France and 17.5 per cent in the United Kingdom, though British breeders were hopeful that steps could be taken to reduce the differential.

Political support has thus complemented the geological, climatic and social benefits of Ireland to ensure that over the last quarter of a century this small country has been one of the world's top Thoroughbred-breeding nations. Some 360 stallions now stand in

Ireland, and the country is home to over 11,000 broodmares (more than in Great Britain), who in 1991 produced 7,300 foals (compared with 5,656 in Great Britain).

We saw earlier how the potential of Ireland as a venue for breeding high-quality horses was recognised in the seventeenth century, and how any hope of a steady development of breeding was damaged by the upheavals of the late seventeenth and early eighteenth centuries before the sport revived around 1730. The early nineteenth century saw distinct signs of attempts to improve the breed, with the running of royal plates – the officially funded races designed to encourage the breeding of weight-carrying long-distance horses – on the increase.

Faugh-a-Ballagh, a full brother to Birdcatcher, was the first Irish-bred winner of an English Classic when successful in the 1844 St Leger: subsequently standing in England, he was the sire of Leamington, who became a top stallion in the USA and himself sired Iroquois, first American-bred winner of the Derby.

In the early years of the twentieth century the most influential Irish sire was Gallinule, who was twice champion sire in England, a feat previously accomplished by only one Irish sire, Birdcatcher himself. Gallinule stood at the Brownstown Stud at The Curragh, near which are located two more of the most important studs of that time. Eustace Loder's Eyrefield was the place of birth of Gallinule's most famous offspring, Pretty Polly, and just off The Curragh on the way into Kildare was William Hall-Walker's Tully Stud.

Colonel Hall-Walker made a huge contribution to the long-term prosperity of Irish bloodstock, but his principles of breeding were a far cry from the Coolmore computers. A keen student of astrology, he believed that the stars exerted an influence on Thoroughbred matings. He ensured that the stallion boxes incorporated skylights through which the horses could view (and presumably be viewed by) the stars, and the casting of horoscopes was an important element in planning matings and deciding whether to sell or keep foals. Yet Hall-Walker was no crackpot. He acknowledged that 'There is no royal road to success in breeding either by the aid of Astrology, Botany or Physiology, but these all have their use if applied in an intelligent manner', and his results spoke for themselves. By the outbreak of the Great War he had bred Cherry Lass, winner of the One Thousand Guineas and Oaks in 1905, Witch Elm (One Thousand Guineas winner in 1907), Minoru (winner of the Two Thousand Guineas and Derby in 1909, leased to King Edward VII) and the St Leger winners Prince Palatine (1911) and Night Hawk (1913).

In 1915 Hall-Walker – who was to become Lord Wavertree four years later – presented all his bloodstock to the British government on condition that it purchase his properties at Tully and in Wiltshire at an independent valuation. For £65,625 Britain acquired the studs along with, at Tully, six stallions, forty-three broodmares (including the dam of the great sire Blandford), ten two-year-olds, nineteen yearlings and some three hundred Shorthorn cattle. The National Stud, as Tully thus became, produced horses such as Blandford, the 1942 Two Thousand Guineas winner Big Game, and Sun Chariot, winner of the One Thousand Guineas, Oaks and St Leger the same year. In 1943 the Irish government claimed Tully, and the British transferred all its stock to Gillingham in Dorset, where the National Stud had its home (with another base later established at West Grinstead) before moving to Newmarket, where the new National Stud was opened in April 1967.

Thus was established at Tully the Irish National Stud, with the objective of providing Irish breeders with the services of high-class but inexpensive stallions. The first stallion bought was Royal Charger, who had a lasting influence: his son Turn-To became one of the top stallions in America and sired Sir Gaylord and Hail To Reason, sires respectively of Sir Ivor and Roberto. Panaslipper, who won the Irish Derby in 1955, stood at the Irish National Stud, as did the Derby winner Tulyar.

Under the wise management of Michael Osborne in the 1970s the Irish National Stud enjoyed a period of marked prosperity, thanks in large measure to Osborne's policy of bringing to the Stud a small group of high-class mares: among the horses bred there at this time was the 1979 Two Thousand Guineas winner Tap On Wood, by Sallust. The year that Tap On Wood won the Guineas, the Stud purchased Ahonoora for £200,000, selling him to Coolmore for £7 million in 1987, by which time he had sired such horses as Park Appeal, Park Express and the Two Thousand

Mares and foals at the Irish National Stud in County Kildare

Guineas winner Don't Forget Me. Ahonoora was bought by Coolmore to stand both in Ireland and in Australia, where he was put down after an accident in 1989 – but not before his last crop in Ireland had included Dr Devious, winner of the 1992 Derby.

Today the Irish National Stud continues its policy of offering domestic breeders good but affordable stallions, and remains an important element of the breeding scene in Ireland. As befits a national institution, it is open to the public and attracts some 90,000 visitors a year. They can see not only the stallions, mares and foals, but also the Irish Horse Museum, with its star exhibit of the skeleton of Arkle, and the remarkable Japanese Garden laid out by Hall-Walker, whose spirit still pervades the place: in the roofs of the stallion boxes are skylights, so that the horses can see the stars.

The Irish National Stud is just off the great plain of The Curragh at the Kildare end. At the other end, near Newbridge, is the Baroda Stud, founded by the Maharajah of Baroda in 1948 to stand his Classic winners My Babu and Sayajirao. And on the way into Newbridge is the Ballymany Stud, part of another of the great breeding empires of the world but now notorious as the stud from which, on the night of 8 February 1983, Shergar was abducted, never to be seen again.

Ballymany is one of two studs in Ireland belonging to Shergar's owner, the Aga Khan, whose grandfather was one of the most important figures in Irish breeding. The old Aga Khan had his interest in racing and breeding whetted by talking to Hall-Walker when visiting Tully in 1904, but he did not start his own breeding operation in earnest until 1921, when he set about buying yearling fillies. His operation in Ireland grew to the point where he had no fewer than five studs there, at which he bred many famous horses – notably the 1935 Triple Crown winner Bahram, Tulyar, winner of the 1952 Derby and St Leger, and the 1950 Two Thousand Guineas winner Palestine. Nasrullah, bred in County Kildare by the Aga Khan, sired such horses as Musidora and Never Say Die before being sold to America, where he was four times champion sire and where he got such greats as Nashua, Bold Ruler – sire of Secretariat – and Never Bend, sire of Mill Reef. Through the transmission of such blood has Irish breeding made its mark internationally.

The current Aga Khan is just one of the big players in the international bloodstock business who have studs in Ireland. Robert Sangster and his partners, as we have seen, have the Coolmore group. Khalid Abdullah has studs in County Meath and County Kildare under the Juddmonte Farms banner. And the Maktoum brothers have extensive bloodstock interests in the country. Derrinstown Stud and Ballygoran Stud in Maynooth, County Kildare, belong to Sheikh Hamdan Al-Maktoum. Sheikh Maktoum Al Maktoum has the Woodpark Stud in Dunboyne, County Meath – a present from his younger brother Sheikh Mohammed, who was finding it too small. Sheikh Mohammed himself now has four studs in County Kildare, principal of which is the Kildangan Stud, near Monasterevin.

A simple visit to the bathroom at Kildangan Stud tells you that you are in no ordinary establishment. Those tiles! Those mirrors! Those gold taps! 'No expense spared' does not express it adequately. 'Money no object' is nearer the mark, and with Sheikh Mohammed, as with few other men in the world, that phrase can be used literally. The opulence extends to the stud buildings, beautifully and expensively constructed from red brick which seems to glow in the sunshine and set in 1,400 acres of the most glorious parkland. But the trees which adorn Kildangan are not just there to create a sylvan atmosphere, for – as at Coolmore – the name of the game is ecosystem: the leaves which fall from the thousands of deciduous trees are left to rot and then harrowed into the pasture, thus enriching the mineral content of the grass.

Sheikh Mohammed acquired Kildangan Stud in 1986. It had been founded by Roderic More O'Ferrall, who constructed training facilities there before taking out a trainer's licence in 1927, only subsequently becoming involved in breeding. A serious investor in racing around the world since the late 1970s, Sheikh Mohammed first turned his attention to Ireland about 1983, realising that the country was an ideal place to have youngstock reared before going into training. He was of course not the first to have come to this conclusion, and in the past large-scale English breeders such as Lionel Holliday and Dorothy Paget maintained Irish studs on which their growing young horses could reap the benefits that the Irish climate and pasture so liberally bestow. Sheikh Mohammed bought Woodpark Stud in Dunboyne, and spent three years having it developed to the required pitch of excellence. But his band of broodmares was rapidly growing, and by 1986 he needed somewhere larger. So he gave Woodpark to his brother and bought Kildangan, later also acquiring the Blackhall Stud at Clane, Old Connell Stud, just outside Newbridge, and the Ragusa Stud at Ballymore-Eustace – all in County Kildare.

In Sheikh Mohammed's hands the existing buildings at Kildangan were completely refurbished and many new facilities built. There are now nine yards for the mares (separate yards reduce the risk of any infection spreading), including an isolation yard. The original yard was preserved but completely overhauled.

The money which Sheikh Mohammed has spent on the refurbishment of Kildangan and the other studs he has bought in Ireland may be the stuff of which minds are boggled, but it has a great and direct significance for the present and future of breeding in Ireland. The investment of breeders like the Maktoums in the infrastructure of the bloodstock business ensures the continuing presence of some of the highest-quality mares in the world – the likes of Pebbles and Oh So Sharp are among the 300-or-so brood-

Shergar parading through the streets of Newbridge in October 1981 before taking up residence at the Ballymany Stud

mares at Kildangan – as well as top stallions, and, no small matter for the local economy, brings jobs to rural areas: Kildangan provides employment for over a hundred people.

But Kildangan is concerned with more than just breeding, and its breaking and training complex adds a further dimension to Sheikh Mohammed's Irish operation. He has installed a one-mile-round all-weather track and this, along with grass gallops, forms the basis of facilities on which yearlings are put through a pre-training routine before being sent off for their formal training. Shaadi, for example, was brought from Keeneland to Kildangan, where he was broken and taught the rudiments before being sent to Michael Stoute. Having won the Irish Two Thousand Guineas and the St James's Palace Stakes, he returned to Kildangan to stand as a stallion. Kentucky-bred Ensconse, winner of the Irish One Thousand Guineas, was broken here before going off to Luca Cumani, and other horses to have learnt the basics at Kildangan include such familiar names as Old Vic and Mtoto. The stud is also used for the rehabilitation of horses in training who have met with a setback: Royal Gait, Champion Hurdler in 1992, spent time here.

Yet for all the money-no-object creature comforts of Kildangan, the Irish bloodstock business is a broad church, and at the humbler end of the spectrum the small breeders continue to form the backbone of the industry. There are plenty of them: around three-quarters of Irish breeders own three mares or fewer. We have seen how the jumping greats such as Arkle and Golden Miller came from unassuming origins to leave an indelible mark on the history of their sport. Then there is Red Rum, bred by Martin McEnery at his Rossenara Stud in County Kilkenny. He sent his mare Mared to the stallion Quorum, standing at the Balreask Stud near Dublin Airport, breeding for speed. Red Rum had speed – he dead-heated over five furlongs as a two-year-old at Liverpool – but entered the tiny field of all-time greats when winning his third Grand National in 1977.

With these famous names we could bracket another of the Turf's immortals, a Champion Hurdle winner but remembered more for the feats at Royal Ascot which lodged him for ever in the hearts of racing fans – Brown Jack.

One of the most popular horses ever to run in England, Brown Jack, foaled in 1924, was bred by George Webb of Corolanty, Master of the Ormond Hunt. Webb took him as a yearling to the Birr Show: 'There were only four yearlings in the class in which I showed him, and when I saw them I thought I was sure of first prize.' Wrong. Brown Jack was judged last of the four. The yearling then went to Goffs sales, but no one made a bid. Outside the sale ring Webb met Marcus Thompson, from Golden, County Tipperary, who decided that he liked the look of Brown Jack, bought him for £110, and took him back to Kilmore, County Tipperary, where the horse spent a restful winter out at grass in the company of a donkey. The following June, Charlie Rogers, of Balfstown Stud in County Dublin, set out for Tipperary to look for potential chasers. One morning, when he was in a hurry to get from the Cashel area to Limerick Junction to see one of his horses running in the first race, Rogers ran out of petrol. He had managed to get himself stranded near Kilmore, so he called at the house, explained his predicament, and persuaded Marcus Thompson to drive him to Limerick Junction. 'On driving down his avenue I saw a horse grazing on the lawn with a donkey and asked what it was. Thompson replied that it was a two-year-old gelding by Jackdaw.' Rogers made Thompson an offer for the gelding, which was declined, but later he increased his bid and took possession of the horse.

Convinced that this was a real racehorse in the making, Rogers followed his Irish instinct: he gave the gelding time, and turned him out for six months on the excellent County Meath grass. Brown Jack went into training in 1927, when he was three, but the months at grass had made him fat and lazy. He woke up somewhat for his first race, at Navan in May, but finished last. Yet he was starting to show promise, and before long he had been sold to the English trainer Aubrey Hastings, who was looking for a horse to win the Champion Hurdle for Major Harold Wernher. Brown Jack seemed to fit the bill, and Hastings bought him for the sum of £750, plus £50 if he ever won a race. By the time he retired Brown Jack had won twenty-five. He took the second ever running of the Champion Hurdle in 1928, and on the Flat became one of those very few horses of which the word 'legend' can be used without apology: he won the Goodwood Cup, the Ebor Handicap, the Doncaster Cup and the Chester Cup, and at Royal Ascot he won the Ascot Stakes in 1928 and the Queen Alexandra Stakes six years running, from 1929 to 1934. Whatever may have happened had Charlie Rogers not run out of petrol, the Brown Jack story is steeped in the atmosphere of Irish breeding.

We have had ample evidence of the strength of National Hunt breeding in Ireland, and the contribution of breeding for jumping to the overall health of the country's bloodstock industry continues to be recognised. The Coolmore group of studs, for example, has a history of National Hunt breeding to maintain. By 1992 Coolmore-sired horses had won the Cheltenham Gold Cup eight times, the Grand National three times and the Champion Hurdle five times, and the group has a fine tradition of National Hunt stallions, including Cottage, Fortina and the legendary – again the word is defensible – Deep Run. Standing at the Grange Stud, Deep Run sired a succession of fine National Hunt performers – Dawn Run, Golden Cygnet, Ekbalco, Morley Street, Waterloo Boy and countless others. He has been champion National Hunt sire in Britain for thirteen consecutive seasons to 1991-2, and although he died in 1987 his influence will live on for a good while yet.

For the Irish still dominate National Hunt breeding. Of the twenty-two designated Grade One races run during the 1991-2 season in Great Britain, twelve were won by Irish-bred horses: Remittance Man, National Hunt Horse of the Year, was Irish-bred, as were the other Grade One winners Bradbury Star, Clay County, Cool Ground, Miinnehoma, Morley Street, Mutare, New York Rainbow, Pat's Jester, The Illywhacker and Waterloo Boy. Of the top

Deep Run at the Grange Stud, County Cork

twenty jumping sires in Britain that season, seventeen – including the first fourteen in the list – were Irish-based. So it is not surprising that as far as the jumping breeders are concerned, the state of the British economy is every bit as important as the state of the Irish. Whereas breeders of horses for the Flat have a worldwide market, by far and away the major export outlet for producers of National Hunt horses is Britain. It is to Ireland that the top English jumping trainers look when buying young horses.

Jenny Pitman, for example, makes regular sorties to Ireland for the horses which will keep her in the front rank of her calling, and you only have to consider a few of her recent Irish acquisitions – 1991 Gold Cup winner Garrison Savannah, Toby Tobias, Golden Freeze, Don Valentino, Royal Athlete – to see what makes her trips worth while. 'Sometimes you get the impression that everyone has got a horse in Ireland. I've seen them in back gardens, in garages, in sheds – everywhere except the kitchen!', she told Geoff Lester for the *Irish Racing Annual*. So why does she do most of her buying in Ireland?

'Why do people fish in streams?'

AROUND THE WORLD

The excellence of Irish-bred racehorses has spread right round the globe, and not just in the main racing countries. The number in 1991 of individual winners racing in different countries that were bred in Ireland or sired by Irish-based stallions shows how far the influence of Ireland has reached:

Country	Individual winners	Country	Individual winners
Australia	10	Jersey	11
Austria	26	Macau	55
Barbados	2	Malaysia	35
Belgium	103	Netherlands	26
Brazil	4	Norway	42
Denmark	44	South Africa	16
France	200 (including 27 Group winners)	Spain	17
Germany	111 (including 16 Group winners)	Sweden	63
Guernsey	4	Switzerland	16
Hong Kong	90	Trinidad	4
Hungary	6	Turkey	3
Italy	572 (including 24 Group winners)	USA	116
Japan	15	Yugoslavia	11

Of the 321 races run in 1991 under the European Pattern in Great Britain, France, Ireland, Germany and Italy, 68 – over one-fifth – were won by Irish-bred horses.

Of the 24 Group One races run in England in 1991, seven were won by Irish-breds.

CHAPTER EIGHT

THE CRACK

AT THE HOTEL KEADEEN, a few hundred yards from The Curragh, the revelry of Irish Derby Day 1992 enters its evening phase as racegoers drift from the course into the hotel grounds to drink in (and drink in) the evening sunshine.

A well-known Dublin journalist meets an old friend from the South and they chat about the bibulous occasion when they last met in the capital. The friend remembers that 'It took us nine hours to get back to Cork.' Nine hours?!? *Nine hours* for a journey of some 200 miles, which would normally take four? Had their car broken down? Had they met freak weather, or desperate traffic? No: they had just taken their time, and enjoyed themselves on the way. It was, the friend elaborates, 'Great crack!'

The idea of 'the crack' is diminished by any po-faced attempt at definition. The crack – *craic* in Irish – is fun, enjoyment, revelling in the occasion. You cannot always set out to find the crack: if it's there, it will find you – surprise you, sometimes. You know when you're having it, and it's not only the hangover that tells you when you've had it. The essential ingredients are a group of like-minded companions predisposed to enjoy themselves in any manner appropriate to the occasion, and a reasonable supply of alcoholic beverage.

The crack is of course not only to be found on the racecourse, but racing and betting form an ideal context, and nowhere is it more enthusiastically pursued than at the National Hunt Festival at Cheltenham every March.

On the Monday of Festival week, a coach is picking up Irish punters at Heathrow, and before moving off the driver checks the hotel destinations of his passengers.

'Coach House?'

'Yes', answer a few.

'Moat House?'

'Yes.'

'Anybody else?'

'Poor house . . .'

That the Irish invade Cheltenham may be a cliché of modern sport, but the invasion is also one of its wonders. Never mind that many of those who flock to the Cotswolds every spring are rarely if ever to be seen on an Irish racecourse: Cheltenham is the great annual expression of the Irish abroad, and their presence gives the meeting its incomparable atmosphere. By plane and by ferry, they pour over in their thousands, many having saved all year – since the day of their return to Ireland the previous March – for those three days of glorious racing and all the surrounding crack in the bars and hotels of that most genteel of English spa towns.

Cheltenham is the essence of the crack – the heady expectation of plotting the touches and planning the bets, the late-night sing-songs and card-schools which all too soon slide into the early morning, getting it wrong and getting it right, losing and winning. 'We'll get in and get our things unpacked in the hotel first,' explains a typical visitor to a radio reporter, 'have our dinner, and as soon as that's over then we'll start to organise something – we'll go for a bit of a ramble around the town – two or three different pubs . . . the sing-song starts about eight o'clock at night . . . we'll end up back in the hotel, and we'll have a game of cards and a few more drinks – it'll be late enough into the morning before we finish – though we might try and make it early the first night – three or four o'clock probably.' The Cheltenham crack is traditionally rounded off on the Friday, the day after the final day of the meeting, with a champagne brunch at the Queen's Hotel.

With all this extra-curricular activity, the wonder is that the invaders have any stamina left for three days of the best racing the winter game has to offer. But they do, and any Irish-trained winner at the meeting – well backed or no – is afforded a rousing reception. Recent moments of Irish rapture at Cheltenham spring readily enough to mind – notably the triumphs of Arkle and Dawn Run – but it was in the decade following the end of the war that Cheltenham established itself as a magnet for Irish punters, and with good reason. In 1946 five races at the meeting (including the

Hands across the water: an Irish congratulation for Mrs Cath Walwyn after Ten Plus had won the Sun Alliance Novices' Hurdle at Cheltenham in 1986

Champion Hurdle and Gold Cup) went to Irish-trained horses, and thereafter it was rare for the Irish not to land at least one of the major races – and the extraordinary regularity with which Vincent O'Brien's runners took one or other (or both) of the divisions of the Gloucestershire Hurdle provided a solid base of funds for the week's crack.

Before long Cheltenham became the natural target for any Irish-trained chaser or hurdler who showed a modicum of promise, and those who actually made it to the meeting were usually accompanied by a phalanx of supporters. On some challengers the Irish were on to a man (and woman); in more open races loyalties would be divided, but any Irish-trained winner storming up the hill would still be greeted by that special roar.

In recent years so many of the best Irish-bred horses have been sold to English trainers that the flow of 'Irish' winners at the Festival meeting has slowed considerably. At the 1992 fixture, just two of the nineteen winners (My View in the Coral Golden Hurdle Final and Montelado in the Tote Festival Bumper) were trained in Ireland. There had also been two victories for Irish trainers in 1991 (when ten of the eighteen winners had been bred in Ireland), and the stories of both triumphs that year, in their very different ways, spoke volumes about the Irish and Cheltenham.

Lovely Citizen, winner of the Christies Foxhunter Challenge Cup, had been bred in Lombardstown, near Mallow, by Eugene and Fiona O'Sullivan. As a three-year-old Lovely Citizen had broken a hock and it was suggested that he be put down, but the O'Sullivans nursed him back to race fitness. The horse displayed his thanks for this tender loving care by learning how to undo the latch of his box, and on one occasion absented himself for two days before returning home. Lovely Citizen was the epitome of the small-time Irish challenger at Cheltenham and in the Foxhunters seemed to have little chance against the hotpot Teaplanter, but the favourite unshipped his rider on the first circuit and Lovely Citizen – ridden by his trainer's brother Willie O'Sullivan – won by a head from Dun Gay Lass, whose jockey had suffered the misfortune of a stirrup iron breaking during a desperate duel with the winner on the run-in. Never mind that there was an element of luck about this Irish victory: 'The Banks Of My Own Lovely Lee' was never sung with more fervour than by those supporters from County Cork who crammed into the winner's enclosure that day.

Whatever those invaders won by backing the 14-1 Foxhunters hero would have been small change to Noel Furlong, whose touch on Destriero in the Trafalgar House Supreme Novices' Hurdle two days earlier had gone straight into the annals of the famous bets. Furlong, a carpet magnate who had reportedly settled the trifling sum of £500,000 with HM Customs and Excise over a VAT demand before he was able to travel to Cheltenham, had bought Destriero out of Mick O'Toole's stable after the gelding had won a Leopardstown bumper. Destriero's first appearance over timber was in a maiden hurdle at the same course in December 1990, and after an easy victory there he was pointed at Cheltenham – and the temptation to pick up a little prize money on the way was resisted, according to his owner, because 'we didn't want to end up getting 2-1 instead of 6-1'. So Destriero tackled the Supreme Novices' Hurdle – the top two-mile novice hurdle of the season – as only the second hurdle race of his life, but he won smoothly under Pat McWilliams to land Furlong winnings which were first reported to be in the region of £3 million, before being scaled down to a more realistic million or so.

But the fun that Tuesday was not over yet, as Furlong also had The Illiad in the Smurfit Champion Hurdle, and his various doubles at fancy odds made the horse a mammoth loser for some off-course bookmakers. Furlong had already landed a big gamble with The Illiad in the Ladbroke Hurdle at Leopardstown – for which the horse had been backed from 33-1 to 7-1 – and stood to scoop around £10 million if he could win the Champion, for which The Illiad's odds had shrunk from 12-1 at the opening show to 11-2 second favourite at the off. But salvation (for the bookmakers) was at hand in the shape of the fourth last hurdle, which The Illiad clouted so hard that his chance evaporated: he came home last of the twenty-one finishers.

Never mind: it wasn't too bad a day for Noel Furlong.

The Gay Future coup, perhaps the most celebrated of all Irish betting stories, is complicated; these are the bare bones.

The brainchild of Cork-based building contractor Tony Murphy, the scheme involved entering a horse named Gay Future in an obscure novices' hurdle at Cartmel on August Bank Holiday Monday, 1974, in the name of the Scottish-based permit-holder Tony Collins. Collins also entered a horse named Racionzer in the same race, and Opera Cloak and Ankerwyke in races at Plumpton and Southwell which were due to start close to the time of the Cartmel race. The 'Gay Future' in Collins's care had been sent over from Ireland at the end of July but was not the 'real' Gay Future at all: he was being prepared in Ireland by Eddie O'Grady, and was shipped over three days before the race, transferred to Collins's horsebox just off the M6 near Kendal, and taken straight to Cartmel racecourse.

On the Sunday evening, the day before the race, members of the 'Cork Mafia' (including the Cork Garda superintendent J. J. McMahon and John Horgan, whose Tirol would trigger such memorable Irish celebration in the Newmarket unsaddling enclosure after winning the 1990 Two Thousand Guineas) assembled in London, and the following day they trawled the betting shops of the capital to put down the money on Gay Future – most of it not in singles but in doubles and trebles involving Opera Cloak and/or Ankerwyke. (Multiple bets are usually perceived by bookmakers as being from mug punters, and would not have alerted them to sustained betting on Gay Future which would have caused them to shorten his price.)

Now came the key stroke. Neither Opera Cloak nor Ankerwyke ran in the race for which he had been entered. Indeed, neither actually left Collins's stable that day. So all those doubles and trebles became singles on Gay Future, and too late the bookmakers realised the extent of their liabilities. There was no 'blower' service to Cartmel that busy Bank Holiday by which the bookies could send money into the on-course market, so they hurriedly sent representatives speeding up there from Manchester. Too late. By the time they arrived Gay Future had won, his generous starting price of 10-1 helped by the stable arranging for significant on-course money to be placed on their other runner, Racionzer (thus giving the impression that Gay Future was the less favoured of the two runners), and by rubbing soap flakes into Gay Future's neck before he entered the parade ring to make it seem that he was sweating up.

Some bookmakers knew a legitimate coup when they saw one and paid up; most, though, did not, and only a fraction of the anticipated £300,000 pay-out was actually collected. The police launched a prosecution, and Murphy and Collins were convicted of conspiracy to defraud the bookmakers and fined.

The Gay Future story did not end in financial success, but it became part of the lore of the Irish and racing. It inspired an excellent book (*The Gay Future Affair* by Larry Lyons) and a wonderful television film (*Murphy's Stroke*, directed by Frank Cvitanovich), and was commemorated by the naming of a cocktail bar – the Gay Future Bar in Cork's New Victoria Hotel.

Whatever view you take of the morality of the affair, it is hard not to applaud the ingenuity that lay behind it. And as Tony Murphy tells a reporter at the end of *Murphy's Stroke*: 'The money didn't matter all that much. It was the crack.'

The crack comes in many forms, and in surroundings as far apart as The Curragh on Irish Derby Day and a rural point-to-point, nursery of so many fine Irish jumpers and jump jockeys: there are around eighty point-to-point meetings in Ireland each year. Visit any Irish race meeting, and the crack will be there.

It was there on the visit of Lester Piggott to Killarney in July 1991, the fulfilment of a dream for the indefatigable Finbarr Slattery, then in his last year as Secretary at the course. A long-time friend and admirer of Piggott, Slattery had kept up a constant correspondence with the jockey while 'The Long Fellow' was in prison, and Piggott's visit to Killarney was an affirmation of a special bond between the two men. A record first-night crowd of nearly six thousand flocked to the picturesque track on the edge of the town – Lester, asked if he had ever ridden in a more scenic setting, conceded: 'I've seen worse' – and soon saw Piggott notch a treble for Vincent O'Brien. The ecstasy with which each of Piggott's wins was greeted left no doubt about the special place he retained in the affections of the Irish.

Irish Derby Day at The Curragh is Ireland's greatest contribution to the calendar of European racing, but to compare it with Derby Day at Epsom or with Royal Ascot or with Arc day at Longchamp is to miss the point. Take it on its own terms – a glorious racing and social occasion – and enjoy the crack.

The weather helps. In 1992 the sun shines brightly. A crowd of 23,177 streams on to The Curragh – more than paid to watch the Derby at Epsom. This may be the showpiece of Irish racing, but the mood is relaxed. Plenty of racegoers have put on their Sunday best (it is, after all, Sunday); others have dressed up more elaborately for the occasion, and certain of the ladies' hats are something to wonder at – but this is not Royal Ascot, and the wearing of a hat is not the point of attending. It has its uses, though, in getting its wearer on to the society pages of Dublin

Lester Piggott and Finbarr Slattery in the winner's enclosure at Killarney in July 1991 after the victory of Defendant

newspapers the following day, where wholesome young ladies in fetching headpieces are shown with captions proclaiming them to be 'out to pick a few winners at the sun-drenched Curragh race-course'.

The combination of sun and society naturally calls for drink, that basic ingredient of real crack, and the somewhat rudimentary champagne bar by the far corner of the parade ring is as a jampot to the society wasps. A humbler drink is not far from the mind of any racegoer, for the Classic itself is sponsored by Budweiser, and a vast inflated can of Bud swings in the breeze in the infield, like some bizarre three-dimensional Andy Warhol creation. The infield itself is named the Budweiser Green for the day, and offers all manner of entertainment, including a funfair, live bands, and (naturally) endless supplies of the sponsor's product.

The Budweiser connection with the Irish Derby underlines the day as a truly international event – the only day of the international racing year when Ireland takes centre stage – and this is reinforced by the presence of plenty of American celebrities from stage and screen: Donald O'Connor of *Singin' in the Rain* fame, Stephanie Powers, John Forsythe of *Dynasty*. Another American visitor is the comedian Norm Crosby, brother of Bing. They still recall at The Curragh how Bing Crosby celebrated the 1965 Irish Derby victory of Meadow Court, in whom he had a share, by giving an impromptu rendition of 'When Irish Eyes Are Smiling' to the crowd in the stands. Somehow the notion of Hamdan Al-Maktoum leading Epsom racegoers through a couple of verses of 'Maybe It's Because I'm A Londoner' fails to ring true.

A ticket tout plying his trade behind the grandstand spots Paul Newman – 'Cool Hand Luke! Whoo! Hallo! I'm buying and selling!' Newman has been brought over by Budweiser to announce the establishment in Ireland of a summer camp for children with cancer and serious blood disorders: Anheuser-Busch, parent company of Budweiser, is making a substantial donation, as are Guinness and other Irish companies. 'I shot a film over here about ten years ago,' says the actor: 'I fell in love with the place then and I'm still in love.'

Another link in the chain connecting the Irish Derby with the USA is provided by the presence of the American broadcaster

Adrian Flannelly, who is covering the events of the weekend live for two million listeners to his New York radio station and many other ethnic Irish radio stations all over the USA and Canada.

As far as the racing is concerned, the key to the afternoon is whether St Jovite, trained by Jim Bolger and ridden by Christy Roche, can reverse Epsom placings with the Derby winner Dr Devious, trained in England by Peter Chapple-Hyam and ridden by John Reid. The build-up to the race has been soured by the controversy of the Turf Club's postponing Roche's appeal against a fifteen-day ban for improper riding at Naas two weeks previously, and the suspicion persists that the authorities have backed down in the face of an implied suggestion from Bolger that he would be reluctant to run the horse in the Irish Derby were Roche not free to take the ride. But few of the crowd basking in the sun are much concerned about the political intricacies of the matter: they know that St Jovite is far and away Ireland's best hope to land the country's top race – and there has not been a home-trained winner since 1985.

The early omens are good. Bolger and Roche take the opening race with Perfect Imposter. The next event is the Sea World International Stakes, sponsored by the Sea World family of marine aquatic parks in the USA, part of Anheuser-Busch. This goes to the English-trained, Italian-owned, South African-ridden and American-bred Sikeston. But Bolger and Roche are back in the winner's enclosure after Ivory Frontier lands the third.

Excitement mounts – and some of the socialisers even manage to tear themselves away from the champagne bar – as the Derby runners emerge from the saddling boxes. After a turn or two round the parade ring they are led out on to the course itself, where in honour of the occasion the track directly in front of the stands serves as the paddock for the Classic. Then there is the calm before the storm as the crowds jam into the stands and the horses make their casual way across the shimmering plain to the start. Eventually, to a great cheer, they're off.

Two of St Jovite's stable companions, Mining Tycoon and Appealing Bubbles, act as pacemakers until the great hope of Ireland takes up the running more than half a mile out and starts to go for home. As the field swings into the straight the predictable pattern of the race is unfolding: St Jovite is trying to stretch the stamina of Dr Devious, and the Epsom winner is poised to take him on. The noise of the crowd has subsided from that cheer as the stalls opened to an animated babble through the early stages of the race, entering a crescendo as the runners approach the straight. Now, with the moment of truth upon them, the spectators seem to hold their communal breath for a second. Just as well, for as John Reid's whip is glimpsed held aloft above the favourite, it's time to work up to a real Irish roar. Dr Devious is in trouble, and St Jovite is not stopping.

Mezzo forte: 'Come on, Christy!'.

Forte: 'COME ON, CHRISTY!!'

Fortissimo: **'COME ON, CHRISTY!!!'**

Christy comes on all right. St Jovite barrels right away from his rivals and keeps up his relentless gallop through a barrage of ecstatic shouting to the line, where he wins by an astonishing twelve lengths.

Hats on Irish Derby Day 1992

It is a mighty performance, but for the Irish racegoers it is much more than that: it is the end of the famine, of seven lean years since a home-trained winner of their top race. They're not going to stint in celebrating the return of a great Irish horse to the world racing stage, and as Roche brings the horse back to unsaddle in front of the stands, the cheers ring loud and long. Then, on a huge podium facing the stand, comes the presentation of the trophy by the Taoiseach, Albert Reynolds, to Mrs Virginia Kraft Payson, the American owner-breeder of St Jovite. She is still clutching the model leprechaun she carries for luck every time she sees her horse run.

The formalities are dispatched but The Curragh remains abuzz. It is not just that an Irish horse has won the Irish Derby (and at 7-2, a handy price for patriots), but that he did so in such a manner that he may just – and a sunny day like today is no time to err on the side of pessimism – he may *just* turn out to be one of the really great horses.

Three more races, two won by Bolger and Roche (Arrikala at 16-1 and Park Dream at 8-1) to bring their tally for the day to a remarkable five. You remember that joke: 'God lives there. He only thinks he's Jim Bolger.'

By the last the racecourse and its patrons are beginning to look a little ragged, and the remaining racegoers are picking their way through a sea of empty Bud cans. As the runners canter to the post a man moves along in front of the grandstand and holds up a giant placard reading 'JOHN 3:7' – that is, you must be born again. This afternoon Irish racing has been.

The sport is over – but not so the crack. The evening is brilliantly sunny and events on the racetrack demand some reflection, so it's over to the Hotel Keadeen to prolong the day. An hour after the last race the place is teeming with people, and after another hour they are still pouring in by the hundred. Peter Chapple-Hyam, John Reid and others of the Dr Devious team have found a quiet corner of the bar in which to discuss what went wrong with their Epsom hero. There'll be another day. Outside, the extensive lawns of the hotel are rapidly disappearing under a blanket of humanity, a great mix of Irish racing folk – owners, trainers, gamblers ('There's yer man who was involved with that sting on the national lottery'), socialites in their finery, ordinary racegoers, refreshing themselves from the bars strategically placed around the grounds. Soon the music starts and a few people begin to dance, tentatively at first and then with more gusto as the throng increases. A jazz band situated on a small dais on one lawn competes with the disco in the huge marquee on another. Stand midway between the two and you experience the curious sensation of 'Won't You Come Home, Bill Bailey?' in one ear and 'Return To Sender' in the other. It feels like the sun will never go down, the music will never stop, St Jovite will never be beaten.

It's been quite a day.

Forty-eight hours on Dermot Weld has changed the neat blue suit of Irish Derby Day for a salmon pink jersey, blue slacks and a panama hat, and the main topic of racecourse conversation is not whether St Jovite is a certainty for the King George but how come there's now a roof on the smaller stand at Bellewstown? There wasn't last year – though it was good crack, and perhaps we can't remember quite right . . .

Bellewstown, about twenty-five miles north of Dublin, has claims

Going down at Bellewstown

to be one of the oldest racecourses in Ireland. It is certainly one of the most engaging, but to experience its charms you have to get your timing right, as there is only one meeting a year – three evenings in early July. For those three days the tiny village rings to the crack. Its two pubs – the Bellewstown Inn and the Cozy Bar – are packed, and two topics regularly find their way into the conversation: the erection of a roof on the main stand, and now on the smaller stand (have these affected the rural charm of the course?) and the Yellow Sam coup, a brilliant touch brought off at the course by Barney Curley and Mick O'Toole in 1975, which involved the commandeering of the only telephone in the place. Good crack.

Bellewstown is one of the few courses left in Ireland with a free outside enclosure. Here there are bookmakers and Tote facilities, as well as a funfair and any number of possibilities for food and drink, and as punters leave the course each evening they are met not only by the traditional sellers of fruit and sweets, but by stalls selling all manner of second-hand goods.

With its backdrop of trees, the infield a mass of gorse bushes, and panoramic views across to the sea, Bellewstown is a wonderfully scenic place, and the course itself has its idiosyncrasies: the turns are tight and the undulations marked, and for about a quarter of the circuit the runners are out of sight of the spectators, who have that extra frisson of excitement when the horses breast the hill on the run for home. Until a few years ago Bellewstown managed without a running rail, which made it a hazardous venue for parents who liked to picnic here with their children.

Yet for all its charm and the ultra-relaxed nature of the occasion, Bellewstown is no place for backwoodsmen. The top trainers and jockeys are in attendance, and the racing is serious. So it should be, with every event sponsored and total prize money for the 1992 meeting in excess of £90,000, making this the most valuable Bellewstown fixture ever. The racing is also mixed, for the Irish predilection for jumping has to be satisfied, even in July. Steeplechasing at the course was given up after 1977 on account of the chases attracting few runners, but a couple of hurdles feature on each evening's programme, and this year there is the added bonus of the visit of Richard Dunwoody for his first ride here.

Of the three evenings, the major is the middle day, Wednesday. This is Ladies' Night, and in their honour a local printer is sponsoring the 'Most Appropriately Dressed Lady' competition. A nice idea – but unfortunately the weather has raised the question of how literally the judges should take the term 'appropriate'. It is freezing cold and windy, and really appropriate dress this evening would be something out of *Nanook of the North*. A few ladies have taken rather incongruous precautions against the cold, fitting under a skimpy summer dress warm leggings, or those long clinging shorts favoured by Olympic sprinters. But in defiance of the weather they scorn Balaclava helmets and sport fashionable hats, many of which must have been seen at The Curragh a few days ago. Eventually the field is whittled down, and in the paddock the winner is paraded. Her prize is a week's holiday for two in a hotel on Mizen Head, Barleycove, County Cork. Hope it's warmer there.

But the crack transcends the weather, and after racing things liven up outside the bar at the top end of the course, at which vantage point you can clench your chattering teeth and gaze across to where the Mountains of Mourne sweep down to the sea.

Six weeks later the racing community grabs its bucket and spade and rattles off towards Laytown for its annual outing to the beach.

Laytown is a unique racing occasion: the only meeting in Europe under official rules where the sport takes place along the strand – on the coast some thirty miles north of Dublin, with those

Mountains of Mourne providing a dramatic distant backdrop. Local tradition insists that the races, first run officially in 1876, were instigated by the parish priest, then quashed for a time by a high-minded bishop. More fool him, for as a racing experience – and for the crack – Laytown takes some beating, and the presence of dozens of priests suggests that clerical loftiness has long since been overcome.

The essential point about Laytown as a racetrack is that it does not exist. The only permanent building at the course is the gents. Even the ladies turns out to be a portable convenience, and the rest of the essential functions of a race meeting – Tote, bar, secretary's office, weighing room (with its wonderfully ancient weighing chair) – are housed in tents or mobile vans. These are situated around the edges of a field above the beach which for the rest of the year is just that – a field. Walk to the far end, to the edge of the grass, and you suddenly have a panoramic view of a great swathe of beach. Today this is the racecourse. It wasn't yesterday and it won't be tomorrow, but this afternoon, as soon as the tide has retreated sufficiently, the course is laid out and harrowed, marked by red flags on tall poles, with just the far bend (a mile from the finish of a left-handed roughly U-shaped track) and the few yards immediately before and after the winning post afforded the luxury of running rail, which is hammered into the sand as soon as the tide allows.

The tides are the crucial element in the timing of the annual Laytown fixture, in terms of both the day itself and the time of day at which the races take place. Once the tide turns the racecourse will rapidly start to disappear, and it is no coincidence that the final event this evening is a straight mile: by then the round course will not be raceable.

This may sound a bizarre way to stage horse racing, yet Laytown is not some quaint curiosity put on for tourists. It is a proper race meeting and attracts the top trainers and jockeys. OK, St Jovite will not be having his Arc prep here, and there'll be no stalls handlers or betting on the photo-finish, but none the less it's the real thing.

Racing is Ireland may be famously non-elitist, but at Laytown there is a very definite barrier – a mesh fence topped by barbed wire. Inside is the field, the enclosure, for which nearly five thousand people have paid to get in. Outside, down on the beach, is free, and crammed with attractions. For about a furlong up the strand there is a swarm of stalls, which on closer examination turn out to be selling anything from food and drink to musical birthday cards ('See if there's one with "The Mountains of Mourne"') and a startling variety of other merchandise. There is a booth offering face-painting. There are bookmakers, who unlike their fellows in the main betting ring in the enclosure can actually see the racing. There are two well-patronised bouncy castles, swings and a primitive roundabout which looks like something from a Hammer Horror film, and all manner of other entertainments. There are stalls offering card games and roulette to keep gamblers going between races. And beyond these stretch along the beach, for as far as the eye can see, ranks of parked cars.

For the true atmosphere of Laytown, you stay down on the sand to watch the sport at close quarters. The runners descend to the beach from the paddock, and many get noticeably more keyed up than they would when emerging on to the course at an orthodox track. Who can blame them, for the huge expanse of the beach – north towards nearby Ulster, south towards Dublin – offers an exhilarating invitation to gallop. They canter along the beach for a while, then return and assemble at the start, marked by a few yards of running rail, and here the glorious informality of the occasion is again obvious as spectators chat with the jockeys while the horses circle. Dispatched by the starter, the runners hammer off towards the Mountains of Mourne, clattering along the sand and every now and then splashing through puddles of standing water. Towards the far end they edge right then make the sweeping left-hand bend, and meanwhile the spectators on the beach have lined the last few hundred yards of the course. As the runners come charging towards them, daredevil children leap out on to the track like latter-day Emily Davisons, nipping back to safety at the last moment. The field gallops by in a snare-drum of noise rather than the bass-drum of horses on turf, and as the horses head for that squirming knot of people by the winning post the spectators further back down the course move on to the track to view from the rear – 'The crowd that closes in behind', in Yeats's poem.

The runners return to unsaddle, and the crowd on the beach

Before the crack at Laytown

disperses until the next race. Children play in the pools of water, teenagers on ponies ride along by the edge of the sea, adults return to the roulette wheel or the bookies. This is a good day for punters, with three favourites coming in. Dermot Weld has a winner, Mick O'Toole a double.

By the time of the second last race the tide is well on the way back in, and delays to starting times have meant moving the flags on the round course. No sooner have the runners in the last pulled up than tractors and trailers chug on to the beach and the dismantling starts. The flags are removed and the winning post and rails uprooted, and the Laytown punters will hardly be into their second pint of Guinness in the nearby pubs before the course will have completely disappeared, to emerge in twelve months' time like Venus from the waves.

But the fun continues. It's still only early evening, and for miles around the pubs are thronged. In one a grand piano is unearthed, and the singing starts. It's a cosmopolitan repertoire – since when was Eric Clapton's 'Wonderful Tonight' a traditional Irish song? – attacked with gusto, but the numbers which really ring in the rafters are home-grown. An old man leaves his pint at the bar to take the piano stool and perform the unusual feat of bashing out 'Danny Boy' in waltz time, 'The Mountains of Mourne' gets an inevitable airing, and before you know it the lights are being turned out, and Laytown, where the course is by now under deep water, is over for another year.

Great crack!

INDEX

70, 145
Grand National 15–16, 17, 19–20, 43, 49, 51–2, 71, *71*, 72, 75, 99, *100*
Greasepaint 130
Gregalach 49
Griffin, 'Mincemeat' Joe 100, 116
Grundy 20, 92
Gubbins, John 17
Guest, Raymond 71–2, 84, 102

Hall-Walker, William (Lord Wavertree) 140–1, 142
Hard Ridden 76, 77, 79
Harkaway 15
Hastings, Aubrey 147
Hatton's Grace 55, **59–61**, *60*, 97, 98, 111, 124, 125
Haughey, Charles 138–9
Hely-Hutchinson, Mark 29, 30
Hennessy Gold Cup 33, 38–40, *38*, 43
Hill, Mrs Charmian 65–70 *passim*
'hobby', the 10
Holliday, Lionel 144
Hughes, Dessie 62, 63
hunting 21–2, 48, 49, 121, 124, 125
Hurry Harriet 128
Hyde, Tim 51

In A Tiff 24
Irish Champion Hurdle 63, 66
Irish Derby 16, 20, 78, 87, 100–1, 108–10, 156–60, *159*
Irish Grand National 37, 49, 50, 98, 118, 122, 124
Irish Horse Museum 25, *47*, 142
Irish Hospitals Sweepstakes 20
Irish National Stud 9, 141–*2*
Irish Two Thousand Guineas 103, 106
Ivyanna 24

Jaazeiro 106, 111
Jack Of Trumps 113
Japan Cup 91–3
Jerry M 39
Jet Ski Lady 130–1
Jockey Club (English) 12
Joyce, James 23

Kauntze, Michael 24, 102
Keogh, Mrs Moya 59, 98
Kerforo 30, 118
Khalkis 89, 128
Kildangan Stud 134, **143–5**
Killarney racecourse *22*, 155–6
Kinane, Michael 62, *76*, 129
Kinane, Tommy 62, 63
King George VI Chase 33, 44–5, *55, 74*, 75
King George VI and Queen Elizabeth Stakes 79, 87, 89, *90*
Kings Lake 106, 111
Knock Hard 98–9, 111, 125
Kooyonga *ii*, 24

Lanigan, Bob 136
Larkspur 20, 102, 105
Last Link 119
Last Tycoon 133
Law Society 111, 134
Laytown 23, 48, 162–5
Leading Counsel 111
Leopardstown, inaugural meeting at 17
Leap Frog 71
Leney Princess 118
L'Escargot **70–2**, *71*
Levmoss **81–3**, *82*
Lomond 86, 105, 135
Long Look 105
Lovely Citizen 152–3

MacCabe, Colonel Frederick 18
McCalmont, Major Dermot 18
McDonogh, Des 61–2, 63
McGrath, Joe 20, 113
McGrath, Seamus 78, 82, 113
McManus, J. P. 113
McShain, John 78, 80, 81
Magee, Sean 113
Magnier, John 95, 96, 102, 135
Maguire, Adrian *114*
Maktoum brothers 24, 136, 144–5
Manifesto 39
Marshall, Bryan 100, 113
Martial 127
Matt Murphy 147
Meadow Court 128
Meneval 111
Mill Reef 143
Mill House 29, 31–6, 38–40, 41, 45, 46, 57, 117
Minoru 141
Mr What 121
Molony, Martin 21, 53, 54–5, 60, 113, **123–5**, *124*
Molony, Tim 61, 99, 113, 123, *126*, **125–6**
Monksfield 48, **61–5**, *62*
Moore, Dan 70–2, 112
Moore, Joan 72
More O'Ferrall, Roderic 144
Mulcahy, John 102
Mullins, Paddy 65–9, 113, *128*
Mullins, Tom 65, 113
Mullins, Tony 65–9, 113
Mullion, J. R. 89
Murphy, Tony 154–5

National Spirit 61
Newman, Gerry 75
Nicholson, David 41
Night Nurse 63
Nijinsky 20, 21, 76, 83, **86–9**, 95, 102, 103, 104, 105, 107, 111, 135, 136
Noblesse 89, 91, *127*, 128
Northern Dancer 86, 105, 107, 110, 134, 135–6

O'Brien, Phonsie 98, 101
O'Brien, Daniel 96

O'Brien, David 108, 112
O'Brien, Vincent 9, 20, 21, 52, 53, *55*, 59, 60, 61, 75, 77–81, 84, 86, 88, 92, **94–111**, 112, 116, 122, 123, 128, 135–6
O'Grady, Willie 28, 113
O'Hehir, Michael 54, 59
O'Hehir, Tony 131
Olympia 118
O'Neill, Jonjo 62, 64, 66, 67, 68–9, *113*, 114
Orby 17, 18
Osborne, Michael 141
O'Sullevan, Peter 79–80, 92
O'Toole, Mick 161, 165
Oxx, John 24

Paget, Dorothy 113, 144
Panaslipper 113, 141
Park Appeal 141
Park Express 131, 141
Park Top 82, 83, 88
Pendil 74
Perris Valley 130
Persian Heights 134
Persian War 64
Persse, Atty 115
Petite Ile 24
Phoenix Park, opening of 17
Pieces of Eight 104
Piggott, Lester 80, *81*, 83, 84–5, *87*, 88, 94–5, 102, *103*, 104, 105, 108, 133, 155–6
point-to-points 28, 65, 96, 115, 121
'pounding matches' 11
Prendergast, Paddy 21, 78, 81, 89, 112, **126–8**
Pretty Polly 16, 140
Prince Regent 39, 48, **49–52**, *50*, 116, 118, 124
Prix de l'Arc de Triomphe 79–80, 81, 83, 88, 92, 105
Proud Tarquin 118

Quare Times 99, *100*, 101, 111, 122
Quorum 146

Ragusa **89–91**, *90*, 128
Rank, J. V. 49, 50, 100, 116, 125
Rare Holiday 130
Red Rum *71*, 72, 133, 146
Reid, John 9, 104, 113
Remittance Man 147
Reynoldstown 27, 49, 77
Roberto 102, 104, 105, 141
Robinson, Willie 29, 32, *34*, 36, 41, 114, *117*, 123
Roche, Christy 9, 108, *109, 130*, 131, 158–9
Roddy Owen 73
Rodrigo De Triano 103, 110
Rogers, Charlie 146
Rogers, Mick 77
Roimond 52, 53, 54, 116
Royal Academy 94–5, 104, 110, 133